This book is for
Edith Viner
and
Mary and Jimmy Robbins

# Left

# Out of Left Field

## Willie Stargell and the Pittsburgh Pirates

**Bob Adelman
and Susan Hall**

THE TWO CONTINENTS
PUBLISHING GROUP

A PRAIRIE HOUSE BOOK

ISBN 0-8467-0127-8

Library of Congress Catalog Card No. 75-43477

First edition.

Printed in the United States of America.

Designed by Arnold Skolnick.

The Two Continents Publishing Group Ltd.
30 East 42 Street
New York, New York 10017

A Prairie House book

## Author's Note

OUT OF LEFT FIELD is an unauthorized account of a baseball season. Neither Willie Stargell nor the Pittsburgh Pirates reviewed the manuscript before publication. There is no way of measuring their reaction to the contents of this book.

We spent eight months taping and photographing the Pirates, from spring training until the final game of the season. Through the players' own language, we have tried to capture the mood of professional ball, played on a gruelling schedule under the exacting demands of public performance. We taped both in formal interview and in more candid moments in the locker room and dugout. After a few months, the natural resistance to "on the record" conversations was broken and people spoke more freely. Candid comments, while often fascinating, are not always literal expressions of what a person means, nor do they represent considered judgment. In this book, they should be taken in the broad context of a life which, for all its external glamour, is fraught with frustration and loneliness. For instance, Mrs. Stargell blurts out that she wishes everyone with sickle cell anemia would die. In fact, Mrs. Stargell is as deeply committed to the sickle cell campaign as her husband, who made this dread disease known to the public and spends much of his time informing the public about sickle cell anemia. Mrs. Stargell expresses her deep love for her husband but is momentarily caught up by a desolate sense that his public life leaves her alone.

Stargell's off season activities as a profoundly committed public citizen have been only minimally mentioned. Due to unfortunate time pressures in the book's preparation, we were unable to detail this important aspect of Stargell as a man. It is unfortunate, because Stargell is as much a leader of the community and an example to youth as he is a baseball hero. While OUT OF LEFT FIELD details his splendid performance as a player and as a teammate, the portrait is limited because it does not amply describe his humanitarian commitments.

Although there is some discussion of women and drugs in this book, Stargell does not participate in either of these off the field activities. The baseball Annie who speaks is not known personally by Stargell, and we met her quite independently. Life on the road is lonely and baseball, like other professional sports, has its camp followers. As far as we know, this girl is on nothing more than speaking terms with the players she mentions. She ranks herself by bragging of her associations and accomplishments.

We were anxious to report Stargell's contract negotiations, but were repeatedly told that this was impossible. Only when arbitration became a fact of baseball life and salary negotiations a matter of public record did Stargell and his attorney reluctantly acquiesce to the publication of this material.

While this book is a true report of what was said, the nature of the spoken word is often hyperbole and caricature. Over a period of time, inhibitions are weakened; people speak from feeling and under the pressure of a very difficult life. Dock Ellis, for instance, is flamboyant and fanciful. Exaggeration is his style. In his discussion of the use of drugs by his teammates, he is not to be taken literally, but rather he suggests the mental stress these men experience as they grind down the stretch. In no way do we mean to say that all, or a substantial number of the Pirates take drugs. Sometimes when Ellis speaks, he is irreverent and outrageous. But personally, he is an extremely perceptive and sensitive man, who devotes himself to helping his teammates and young ballplayers, a man who is deeply committed to the Pittsburgh community.

We hope to achieve the tone of a season, but the reader must be aware that many statements included in the book are for the creation of mood and not to be taken either literally or out of context.

OUT OF LEFT FIELD is a complex portrait of a unique man and of a team. Stargell is a hero, but he is a human hero. The book was created in this spirit.

**Bob Adelman & Susan Hall**

## STARRING THE PLAYERS

| Pitchers | Born | Birthplace | 1972 Won | Lost | ERA |
|---|---|---|---|---|---|
| Blass, Stephen | 1942 | Canaan, Connecticut | 19 | 8 | 2.48 |
| Briles, Nelson | 1943 | Dorris, California | 14 | 11 | 3.08 |
| Ellis, Dock | 1945 | Los Angeles, California | 15 | 7 | 2.71 |
| Giusti, David | 1939 | Seneca Falls, New York | 7 | 4 | 1.92 |
| Hernandez, Ramon | 1940 | Carolina, Puerto Rico | 5 | 0 | 1.67 |
| Johnson, Robert | 1943 | Aurora, New York | 4 | 4 | 2.95 |
| Kison, Bruce | 1950 | Pasco, Washington | 9 | 7 | 3.26 |
| McKee, James | 1947 | Columbus, Ohio | Charleston (Pittsburgh) | | |
| Moose, Robert | 1947 | Export, Pennsylvania | 13 | 10 | 2.91 |
| Rooker, James | 1942 | Lakeview, Oregon | Omaha (Kansas City) | | |
| Walker, James Luke | 1943 | De Kalb, Texas | 4 | 6 | 3.39 |

| Infielders | Born | Birthplace | AB | R | H | HR | RBI | Pct. |
|---|---|---|---|---|---|---|---|---|
| Alley, Leonard Eugene | 1940 | Richmond, Virginia | 347 | 30 | 86 | 3 | 36 | .248 |
| Cash, David | 1948 | Utica, New York | 425 | 58 | 120 | 3 | 30 | .282 |
| Gonzales, Jose | 1950 | Arecibo, Puerto Rico | 2 | 0 | 0 | 0 | 0 | .000 |
| Hebner, Richard | 1947 | Boston, Massachusetts | 427 | 63 | 128 | 19 | 72 | .300 |
| Hernandez, Jacinto | 1940 | Matanzas, Cuba | 176 | 12 | 33 | 1 | 14 | .188 |
| Robertson, Robert | 1946 | Frostburg, Maryland | 306 | 25 | 59 | 12 | 41 | .193 |
| Stennett, Renaldo | 1951 | Colon, Panama | 370 | 43 | 106 | 3 | 30 | .286 |

| Catchers | Born | Birthplace | AB | R | H | HR | RBI | Pct. |
|---|---|---|---|---|---|---|---|---|
| May, Milton | 1950 | Gary, Indiana | 139 | 12 | 39 | 0 | 14 | .281 |
| Sanguillen, Manuel | 1944 | Colon, Panama | 520 | 55 | 155 | 7 | 71 | .298 |

| Outfielders | Born | Birthplace | AB | R | H | HR | RBI | Pct. |
|---|---|---|---|---|---|---|---|---|
| Clines, Eugene | 1946 | San Pablo, California | 311 | 52 | 104 | 0 | 17 | .334 |
| Davalillo, Victor | 1939 | Cabimas Edo Zulia, Venezuela | 368 | 59 | 117 | 4 | 28 | .318 |
| Oliver, Albert | 1946 | Portsmouth, Ohio | 565 | 88 | 176 | 12 | 89 | .312 |
| Parker, David | 1951 | Cincinnati, Ohio | Salem (Pittsburgh) | | | | | |
| Stargell, Wilver | 1941 | Earlsboro, Oklahoma | 495 | 75 | 145 | 33 | 112 | .293 |
| Zisk, Richard | 1949 | Brooklyn, New York | 37 | 4 | 7 | 0 | 4 | .189 |

# Warming Up

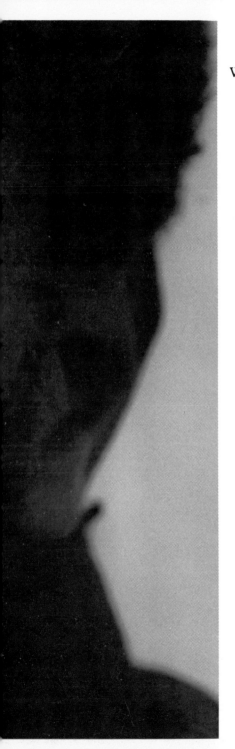

Willie: I'm just raring to go. It's that time of year. All the guys are signing and I've got the itch. My body won't sit still no more.

Last fall, I washed out baseball, hung it up to dry, and then put it away. Now I'm ready to dust! I can't wait to get back behind the plate, because I just love to swing. I want to test my powers. All of a sudden, I'm getting to be an old man. I am only three years from being in my twenties. Not so long ago I was in high school, but in baseball, life is short. I know I am not going to play forever and that's hard to accept. I can't afford to think about my physical powers. I just rely on them. It would take me three years to realize they're gone.

When you start as a ballplayer, you've got everything physical going for you and nothing mental. Baseball is so much a mental game that you don't really peak until you've got some mental control and knowledge of the game. For the past few years, I've felt both physical and mental control. I suppose eventually your body won't perform and it's over.

Maybe Willie Mays played too long, but that's because he was one of the greatest all-around baseball players ever. He could run, hit, throw, catch. He had instincts on the field. You get all these categories, and if you have got seven out of ten functioning well, then you have enough experience to compensate for the other three. Fans hated seeing Willie drop a ball in center field, but I understand. Willie must have felt like I do—that he had enough experience to make up for the loss of some of his powers.

People like us is afraid to leave ball. What else is there to do? Here we are in our thirties and we're dead. What do we have to look forward to? When baseball has been your whole life, you can't think about a future without it, so you hang on as long as you can. Way beyond the time you should probably quit. It's an embarrassment, but you've got to prove to yourself beyond a doubt that you can't play any more. If your teammates and the fans find it sad, at least you can say to yourself, "I'm through." So what if everybody else decided that long before?

I concentrate on positive thoughts when I'm getting ready to go to spring training. First of all, I have to take a week to sell myself in contract negotiations. Even though it's not easy for me to get up for them, I'm always anxious to leave winter and home, so I want the contracts signed and done. I'm proud, which makes it hard for me to talk about my accomplishments. But I do believe in myself, so I go ahead.

Now I go to negotiations with my lawyer. It used to be that the general manager and the manager provided a father figure for us players. When we started coming with lawyers and agents, it was like having your daughter get married. Management felt they were our parents and they were shattered when we'd come in and say, "You're not giving me enough money." Players are becoming more like independent contractors and we're getting more equality with the club people.

It's a tradition of baseball not to tell your salary. I don't know whether this is good for the players, but I'm sure it's good for management.

**For the past two years, Stargell has negotiated his contract with a lawyer, David Litman. Most of the meetings with Joe Brown, the Pirates' general manager, are held with all three parties present. Litman recalls the 1972 negotiations.**

Litman: At our first meeting with Brown, we began talking about the Black Athletes Foundation, an organization to promote knowledge about sickle cell anemia. Willie is the president and had spent a lot of time raising funds during the past winter. Ultimately Brown said, jokingly, "It's time to get down to money and you had a terrible year."

Stargell then said he had talked to his wife and they had concluded that Willie belongs with a certain class of ballplayers. His job with the club was to drive in runs and to maintain the image of the club. He didn't look at his job only as an employe. He had love and dedication to his position with the club. Before the 1972 season began, he had vowed a great year for himself.

Brown: Sure was.

Willie: And I'm going to make a great year in 1972. But I have talked to a group of players of the superstar status, like Torre and Aaron, and I don't feel right in their company. They carry a certain confidence that I can't. I need money to be with Aaron and the others man to man. When I'm in their presence, I know I am not in that class, even though I feel I belong. I would like to know that everyone else feels the same way. The money I'd like is not out of the question. But to have another year like last year, I would have to apply myself and I will.

Brown: No question about that. I have told you how proud I was of you. Even though your legs were bothering you, there was never an alibi. I wish the other players could follow your example—the way you carried yourself and the impression you made. I myself would like to have that kind of stature.

Willie: The toughest part of baseball is to sell yourself or even put a dollar sign on your worth. But in view of everything I've studied, the last time anyone had a year like mine was twenty-one years ago when Ralph Kiner was with the club. I pride myself on my accomplishments, so I have a hundred-thousand dollars in mind.

Brown: You're hurting me.

Willie: I feel I belong in this class. This is my eleventh year.

Brown: I don't mind getting you in the superstar category, but from my standpoint, the raise you asked for is too much. It is better than a twenty-five-thousand-dollar raise based on one good season.

Willie: But Mays received a substantial raise after one exceptional season. Howard got his raise when his team went nowhere.

Brown: I am not familiar with the American League. But almost all the hundred-thousand-dollar players have had four or five outstanding years.

Willie: Seaver is making a hundred-fifty-thousand and he only had one good year. In order for me to build a framework in my mind, I have to have money as an indication. How much to you have in mind?

Brown: I was thinking of eighty five thousand. One way that players get what they want is consistent high-quality performance. One year is not enough. Brock for several years has had more than a hundred runs and stolen fifty bases.

Willie: I sit down and talk to various guys, because I like to know their feelings. Maury Wills advised me, "You go out and get a little extra and you do a little better." Now, money is tiny, but you find that little things are important. I get pleasure when I give presents to my children, and, in return, my children do little extra things for me without my asking.

**Stargell ended up with a contract worth just over $100,000 in 1972. David Litman goes on, now reading from his notes on the 1973 contract negotiations.***

Litman: After forty-five minutes of discussion of travel in Mexico, Brown asked Willie, "How much money am I going to pay you if I let you play for me?" Willie said he just wanted to get to spring training. He referred to the death of Clemente and said it was going to be a hell of a job to keep the club together, without Clemente on the team.

Brown then said, "What do you have in mind, Willie?"

Willie: I'd like to explain. I thought my year was good. Each year I improve on a consistent basis in different ways. I believe I should earn in the neighborhood of one hundred fifty thousand.

Brown: Ugh. That hurts.

Willie: There are a number of things I am trying to do with my life. In many ways, since last month when Clemente died, I have learned that a person has to live. There are things I should do now that I owe to my family. These things cost money. The years I have spent here in Pittsburgh have been a financial struggle. I didn't get paid much when I first came up to the majors. I pride myself on driving in runs and hitting home runs. I have done my job. I got twelve hundred dollars when I signed.

Brown: That doesn't enter into it.

Willie: It does, because this is now my eleventh year in the big leagues. I was pleased with my negotiations last year and I hope to be pleased with them this year.

Brown: I'm sure you won't be, because I don't believe you should get a fifty-percent increase over last year. You had a slump in the playoffs, because you

* The figures in these negotiations were not confirmed by either Stargell or Litman. The reader may draw his own inferences about their accuracy from the 1974 negotiations.

continued to pull the ball. You wouldn't have done that if Harry Walker [former Manager of the Pirates] had been in Pittsburgh. You attempted to hit to left field and you were overstriding and late-hitting.

Willie: I appreciate your criticisms, because I'm not able to see many things myself. I want everyone to give me an opinion about how I play.

Litman: Willie then asked that a substantial portion of his salary be paid on signing so that he could immediately invest and place a down payment on his new home. Brown said he would talk to his principals and let us know. He discontinued the discussion and said that although he did not believe that Willie had had a great year, he felt it was more than a good year and we should find a salary somewhere in between.

Willie told Brown that he had heard Steve Carlton's salary was well above his. Brown said that he had spoken to the general manager involved and found that the recorded salaries were not correct.

The second meeting started with another fifteen-minute discussion on Clemente. Brown said, "I have to go to Puerto Rico. Send me off happy."

Willie: We have to come to an agreement between your twenty-percent raise and the raise I had in mind and really expected.

Brown: As I mentioned before, I'm not using percentages as much as last year. When a player gets higher in the pay bracket, the percentages are necessarily lower.

Willie: The more money you make, the less you make because of higher taxes.

Brown: But the team lost money last year.

Willie: There are certain things I think about: I hit over thirty home runs and my request for salary is not ridiculous. I bust my ass as much as anyone and they make more money than I do.

Brown: Everybody goes through that in their early years.

Willie: But I have got to feel that my efforts are being compensated now.

Brown: A sixty-thousand-dollar raise in two years is compensation.

Willie: But I'm worth more than a twenty-thousand-dollar raise this year.

Brown: You may be worth more than a twenty-thousand-dollar raise, but the front office feels that that is the amount you are worth.

Willie: There must be a happy medium where you'll be happy and I'll be happy.

Brown: I'll be happy no matter what!

**After the second meeting, Stargell decides to reduce his salary request to $135,000.**

Brown: I'm not happy with a hundred thirty-five thousand.

Willie: I've always felt that at negotiations both parties should come away happy.

Brown: We can't always do that. I have just looked back and realized that you received an increase of seventy-two thousand in two years. I can't believe that is not recognition of your production.

Willie: I think it is, but, although I don't want to put myself in a special position, I am always in the top five in the Most Valuable Player voting and there are people who are not and still move into a higher salary category than me.

Brown: I don't know who!

Willie: Well, Crawford after one good year. I break up a game and have the pressure of the team on me all the time.

Brown: I only differ with the dollar evaluation. There are several things which are important; the MVP is only one of them, however, it has been true that for the last two years, you have been a superstar.

Willie: I feel too that I could have had other super years if I hadn't been at Forbes Field [the old Pirate stadium].

Brown: That can't be a basis of negotiation.

Willie: But if I had played at Three Rivers Stadium for my whole career, I might have had five hundred home runs.

Brown: That's conjecture. I measure your production by what you actually did. I feel very strongly that a hundred twenty-five thousand is both substantial and fair in every way, except you want more. There are a couple of differences from last year, because last year the Pirates were champions and this year they were third best.

Willie: That's why I didn't come in here with a higher figure.

Brown: I have never cried poor mouth. I never said we don't have the money, and I'm not telling you that now. But there should be recognition of the difference between '72 and '71. The mere fact that we didn't get into the World Series cost us one million dollars. I can't continue with substantial raises. Last year I paid you more than I wanted, because you wanted to be a hundred-thousand-dollar player. I thought that meant a lot to you. But your year in '72 was not as good as '71.

Willie: I agree, but very few people have ever had as good a year as I had in '71. If I'm going to go out and bust my ass, I want to be happy.

Brown: I told you many times that as long as I feel I've been fair . . .

Willie: I'm not trying to be happy. If I were to be completely happy, I would have to have one hundred and fifty thousand. I'm just trying to be fair.

Brown: The same for me.

Willie: There's ten thousand dollars difference between us. What is the best thing to do now?

Brown: Sign your contract.

Willie: Then we're not in happy agreement. What if I have a great year and get MVP and you come up with only twenty-five thousand.

Brown: Twenty-five thousand is a hell of a raise. It's not minimal. It's substantial.

Particularly on top of the fifty-three-thousand raise you've been offered for the past two years.

Willie: I can not sign for a hundred twenty-five thousand and go to spring training with enthusiasm.

Brown: I don't think enthusiasm can be changed. That's a problem you have to resolve for yourself. With very few exceptions, what happens in negotiations does not affect the player's performance.

Litman: I then met with Brown alone and explained that we would not take less than a hundred thirty thousand. I told him Willie was going to go West to visit his parents or go South with a signed contract. Brown indicated that he did not believe Willie was as upset as I said and he would like to hear from Stargell himself. I told him he was perfectly welcome to call Willie and meet with him to satisfy his curiosity.

Willie met with Brown and substantiated what I had said. We all met again that afternoon in Brown's office and he gave us a hundred and thirty thousand. Brown said, "I hope to receive credit from you for doing this."

*David Litman   Joe Brown*

**At the conclusion of negotiations, Willie reflects on the terms of a baseball contract, the personal costs of being a star, and the high price paid by a young black player entering the game.**

Willie: When I was first approached by the club, I was seventeen. They offered me a thousand. My stepfather said, "No, it's twelve hundred or he stay at home." So they paid twelve. We thought we really took advantage of them!

Players have no flexibility at all in their contracts. Baseball couldn't exist without the reserve clause, but I feel there should be certain modifications. If the player is considered for trade to another club, he should sit in on negotiations. If I were traded to San Diego for a half a million dollars, *I* am the subject for the trade. They are paying money for me, but I don't get a dime of it. I think I should. I would like to be offered to other clubs only at my suggestion. I'm not against being traded; sometimes a change of atmosphere does a player good. I don't know, because I have always been with the Pirates, but I don't think I would hit rock bottom if I left. I sure wouldn't break apart.

I want to be an individual. I don't find now that my contract with the team conflicts with my individuality. My problem is with people in general. As a ballplayer, I'm not looked at as a man. I am just another star with no liberty. For instance, I could sign autographs twenty-four hours a day. If I didn't want to sign an autograph one time, even though I'd been at it all day, I'd be talked about as a difficult guy.

I went to Manchester, Vermont, last winter. I got there about one in the afternoon. Before the banquet, I signed autographs. During the banquet I signed autographs, and after the banquet I signed autographs. At one o'clock at night, I went to have a drink at a private party. This lady came up to me and said, "If I don't have your autograph for my kids, I can't go home."

I said, "Well, ma'am, you can have my room. I'm not signing any more." She couldn't care less about me signing autographs all day. I wanted to enjoy the evening like everyone else. But as players we have no rights.

The hardest thing is to say no nice. When I take my kids to the zoo or an amusement park, the moment I'm recognized, I don't see my kids. When fans say we have no private life, I say no. I'm no better than anyone else, but they are not better than me. I deserve the right to be private sometimes.

Looking back, I've always wanted to be myself. In the ninth grade, I decided to be a doctor, but the school people said I had to take shop and learn to be a carpenter. When I was coming up, I would go down to the lumberyard near the project where I lived. I'd get me some old two-by-fours, whittle them down to a bat, throw up rocks, and hit them. Other kids just threw rocks through windows.

I won't say I didn't do bad things too. I'd break into box cars on the railroad track and take fruit. At a peanut factory, I used to steal raw peanuts and roast them at home. I'd steal plums off other people's trees. This was in Oakland, California, where I grew up.

My mother was lovable and easygoing, but she was always firm about the way she wanted her children to be. My father went on drinking binges and I guess that's why my parents fell out when I was about six. I was sent to live in Florida with an aunt until my mother could get herself together. I remember the old, dark school and bad dinners. I had chores to do around the house, but I always found time for baseball. They used to call me "Lefty milkshake," because I was left-handed and drank milkshakes to fill me up. My big hero in baseball wasn't a black man. I loved Stan Musial, because he was left-handed like me!

In Florida, I wasn't particularly aware of segregation, but when my mother got herself remarried and brought me back to California, I felt like a bird that could fly. I had been living in an all black section of town where the houses were wooded and the roads dirt. Now I was back in the projects with people of all colors. It was a completely different atmosphere. I felt free.

I still had chores to do around the house. My mother fixed hair during the day and worked in a cannery at night. She was gone all the time. My stepfather worked hard too. I was supposed to maintain the house while they were away, but I was always tempted to play baseball. One afternoon, my father came home to find my sister running around alone. I was supposed to be watching her. When I finally came back, I got whipped with a big oak stick for not staying at home.

Nothing could take away my deep urge to play ball. When there were no games going, I'd take a broomstick handle and throw a ball up in the air. I used old ax handles to hit the ball real far. One day a policeman came to the project and formed a police baseball league. He would pass out big old uniforms that didn't fit, but I prided myself on having one, because I'd seen uniformed ballplayers. I felt like a million dollars in that suit. We'd play on Saturdays against other neighborhood teams. The policeman always took time to teach us the fundamentals of the game. They were good fundamentals, but not the best, and my lack of foundation caught up with me later.

By the time I was ten, I'd gotten a newspaper route. My papers were to be delivered no later than five in the evening, but I was also supposed to play grade school softball. If I delivered my papers on time, I couldn't play softball. Since my first love was ball, I'd play and then deliver papers. My mother got complaints from the newspaper supplier. They all thought I was out doing bad. When they found out I was just playing ball, they realized how serious I was. From that time on, I got my parents' complete support. Because they worked two jobs, I still had to keep the house. To this day, I'm pretty good at scrubbing floors. I just didn't identify with that work as a kid. I wanted to be out with my friends.

One time we were Peeping Toms. We ran across an Oriental fellow with a two-way radio set. We didn't know what he was doing, so we spied on him. I could barely see through the curtains of his window. He got a trunk out from under his bed, opened it, and read from a pamphlet, sending messages. For the hell of it, we called the police. Turned out he was a spy, although I don't know for who. We thought it might be the Chinese.

As I grew older, I was exposed to everything any average black kid gets to see. Pimps and con men, dope pushers and gamblers. I could easily have taken the wrong road, but I always wanted to be a baseball player.

My parents were there to push me and guide me the right way. I began to take my own road. Gets to a certain point where you take the training wheels off the bicycle and learn how to balance yourself. Pretty soon, you're riding alone. When you run up against obstacles, you make it through or you don't. I could never be stopped.

In high school, I liked football most, but I had bad luck. In my sophomore year, we had a dummy scrimmage and I was the middle linebacker. The whole offensive line keyed on little me. They destroyed me in one play. I had a chipped kneecap and my leg was put in a cast. The next year, I dislocated my knee when the fellow covering me came down as I went up for the ball. That ended my football career.

During the summer, I began to play in various baseball leagues. One time there was an all-star game in the old Oakland Oaks's park. I remember hitting a double that was the big hit of the game. When they picked a Babe Ruth all-star team to play in Austin, Texas, I wasn't chosen, though I thought I should have been. I was terribly hurt.

After my first year in college, I signed with the Pirates. The Yankees and the Phils were interested, but they wanted me to stay in college for another year to see how I did. I was too eager to play ball. I was only eighteen and the twelve hundred dollars they offered to sign me looked mighty big!

From the beginning, I was disappointed. I went into baseball with high hopes that were soon struck down. My minor-league career was sad. In the small towns where I played, people treated me like a dog.

I had never run into discrimination until I started playing ball, so at first I thought it was something just directed at ballplayers. My first year in the minors, 1959, I was in Texas. I was threatened with a shotgun next to my head by a man who said, "If you hit in the game tonight, I'll kill you." I had to sleep in a car. I had to go to a store and eat bad food. I could have said, "Hey, if I'd known it was going to be like this, it ain't worth it." I almost did give in. It was a lot of pressure for an eighteen year old.

In Texas, it wasn't easy by no means, but I had this deep love for ball. I had always read the box scores in newspapers for motivation. I thought all you had to do was play the game, having no idea that the only time you have fun is when you're out there playing ball. Off the field, I had a very, very high price to pay.

Black players couldn't live with the whites. I lived on back porches in fold-up beds. Other blacks I saw worked in the fields all day until white people came to cart them off. Coming up in California, my people drove cars and lived in their own apartments. We were poor, but we felt there was a way out. In Texas, blacks couldn't eat in restaurants. We'd be put in the kitchen and handed scraps of food in napkins.

I was still expected to go out and perform like anyone else. We'd be traveling ten or twelve hours on the bus and sometimes stop for food on the highway. I wasn't allowed to go in the restaurant. The boys would spend an hour and a half eating chops and steaks. All I could do was have them bring me a lousy cheeseburger. My system got all twisted up.

I don't know how Jackie Robinson survived. I got it before and after the ballgame, but not from the players, like he did. Some white players didn't give a damn and some were sympathetic. A few guys just couldn't come out and accept me as another ballplayer. "Blacks don't want to work for anything. They want to be given everything. Blacks are lazy and drag their feet. Sleepy all the time."

One ballplayer told me that his parents had brought him up to really hate blacks and to learn that we were not their equal. But after he got to know me, he called me aside and said he really disagreed with his mother and father, because I was no different from him. "I like you, and I don't give a damn what color you are. I'll never bring my children up to hate blacks." That meant a lot to me.

When I went back home after the season, my mother didn't recognize me. I weighed about one hundred forty pounds because of my backdoor diet. I was very weak. I was willing to give up what I'd worked for, because I didn't think I could face that racial treatment again. I didn't want to play another year. I started backpedaling.

That winter I worked at a Chevrolet plant to make some money, and I thought a lot. I knew baseball was my way out of the ghetto. I didn't want to always live in projects and poverty. I wanted to be a major-league ballplayer. It dawned on me that if I gave up ball, I'd be going back and it would affect me for the rest of my life.

While I was home, all the rookies in the minors played together. It was like a professional Little League. I found I performed better, because I was eating good food and I didn't have the racial pressure. That helped put some of the burden away.

I didn't look forward to going back to spring training, but I was at least prepared for the trouble. I was determined that nothing and no one could keep me from doing what I wanted to do. I knew that people did make it from the minor to the major leagues. It wasn't an impossible dream. It wasn't like I was going to jump off a building, flap my wings, and fly. I knew if I applied myself, it was possible to make it, no matter what color I was.

When I went to Grand Forks, North Dakota, in that second year, I figured I had left the South and was on my way. My first day in town, I was walking down the street and a man drove by, really staring at me. When he passed me, he was still looking back over his shoulder. As I continued to walk, a little girl and her mother stopped abut fifty feet away. The little girl said, "I want a teddy bear just like that for Christmas."

People who had heard about blacks in Grand Forks didn't want nothing to do with us. One bar in town had a sign: "No Indians, No Niggers Allowed." In that order! I'd go to a restaurant with two Latin players, and when they said, "No niggers," we'd all start speaking Spanish, which I didn't speak. They thought I was some special kind of nigger, so they let me eat.

By 1961, I had gone to Asheville, North Carolina, for my next-to-last year in the minors. I enjoyed playing in that league, because we were in bigger cities, which meant that black people were living there. The smaller the town, the fewer the blacks, and the less position they had. In bigger towns, blacks were able to do things for themselves. The whole situation in the South wasn't like Texas! We stayed in the black community in Asheville where I enjoyed the food. In Knoxville, they had top entertainers coming through and we could join them at the clubs. I was having fun, and improving my game too.

I was in the minor leagues for four years. I needed it. My first two years, I was really at a loss as a player. I had ability, but I didn't play the game as well as guys who'd had some training. Had I been properly educated in baseball, maybe I would not have needed the four years to grow. I started as an erratic thrower and a free swinger. If the ball was at my head, I'd swing. If it was in the dirt, I'd swing. Especially with two strikes on me. I slowly learned control. I was becoming a ballplayer. At the end of my last season in the minors, I was called up by Pittsburgh. I remember my first time at bat. Stu Miller was pitching, and Dick Stuart told me, when I went up to pinch hit, "Don't feel bad when you strike out," and I did.

I've often wondered what it would have been like if I'd said the hell with it. I'd probably be in California messing around in the ghetto. But now I was up in the majors and I could see shore. I was proud of myself more than anything. I had made it out.

I have met so many guys who have been broken by discrimination. I felt sorry, because they were so talented. Two or three were tremendous athletes with more ability than I have, but they couldn't handle the pressure and I don't know what they're doing now. I put my blinders on, blocked out the pressures, and played ball.

Even today I'm made to feel sensitive about my color. I don't get television commercials like the white players, although I use the same products they do. The front office has never talked to me about a job with the club when I retire. I watch management favor white players on the team. I still control myself in baseball.

I have learned to find outlets for the discrimination I run into off the field. I know that you can only put so much water in the pot, so much air in the balloon. Nature has it's own way of doing things. If you put too much air in a tire, it explodes. You try and be calm, but if it happens too often, you jump like a leopard or a panther. You strike back and you strike hard. You hit me and I hit back. Soft, but deep.

For example, if I were walking down a hotel stairway and some man said, "Nigger, what are you doing in this hotel?" I'd say, "Looking for a job." Make a joke of it. My first reaction is to hit him on the head, but I wouldn't give him the satisfaction to know that he'd gotten to me.

When a person calls me *boy,* I say, "Did you say Roy, sir?" If he comes back and says, "I meant boy," then I usually say, "Your mammy has nuts." I know what he said and I let him know I meant what I said.

I was standing by a newspaper stand and two fellows were talking. One said, "Hey, nigger, what are you doing here?" I pretended I didn't hear him. So he says it again. He turns to the other fellow and says, "He heard me." So he says again, "Hey, nigger, what are you doing here? You heard me."

I turned and said, "You're not my brother."

He says, "What do you mean?"

I said, "Well, most of my brothers call me nigger. You going to be my brother?" This blew his mind. He hurt me, yes. But what I said put it all back on him and he turned red in the face and walked away. That gave me satisfaction. After all these years, I've learned to confront racism directly. I can let my anger out without losing control of myself. Home runs are like that too. A lot of feeling focused on the bat.

I didn't start by hitting home runs. When I began to play professional ball, I thought I was Mr. Big until someone told me, "Hey. You have to learn how to hit." When I found out there were techniques, I flipped in a bad way. I had thought I was a natural. I thought they were criticizing me personally. Then I realized that the coaches didn't want to make me someone else's man. They just wanted to help me play ball. I'd had no good fundamentals instilled in me. So I started to learn to control my swing. When I got control, I could use my power. That's how I found one outlet. Through control. But if I don't get a hit for a few games, I can feel the bubbles boiling!

**Willie discusses preparations for the season during spring training at Pirate City in Bradenton, Florida.**

Willie: When I drive down to training, I like to take my time, see my old friends. I am slowly getting away from the winter. My mind is orientating to Florida and what I want to do this year.

I remember coming to spring training in 1962. I almost got killed. Another player and I was driving on a two-lane, divided highway. We were trying to pass another car, but it seemed dangerous on this road. We stopped to get some gas, and, as we pulled out, five highway patrolmen stopped us. They told us we were *molesting* two white women. Apparently the car we'd been hugging had two white women in it, but we didn't know.

The police said, "We're going to take you downtown and in three minutes you'll be dead." I thought we'd had it. As we were driving into town, one policeman finally said, "Where you niggers going?" We said we were ballplayers on our way to spring training. They said, "That's a joke. Prove it." So we open the trunk where we had the baseball gear.

When they saw the bats and gloves and shoes, they let us go. "You just don't molest our white women down here, boys." We were saved by being ballplayers. God knows how many unknown people die that way. We drove for another three and a half hours without saying a word. I was just glad to be alive. I kept it all inside.

Now it's different. I take a leisurely route south, driving with some friends, and when I'm not laughing and visiting, I think about what I'll work on this spring, training.

People don't realize that you have to get in training for hitting and throwing. Baseball is not a natural sport. You have to condition yourself. We're like diamonds in the rough at the beginning of spring training. In the six weeks we're down in Florida, we polish the diamonds. At the completion of spring training, if a guy's had a healthy spring, he can encourage his talents for that year.

When I haven't been swinging the bat for six months, I can see the ball, but I'm not coordinating with my hands. I have to force myself to react until it becomes absolutely natural. I can be seeing the ball good, but I forget to swing. When I hit, my hands are lazy. If one hand is lazy, the other begins to lag. If I'm cocky and my hands are coming through at the same time, I know how I'm going to hit. Both hands have to hit together. One pushes and the other pulls. If a hand is stale, it won't function at all.

I want to hit left-handers to left field this year. I have started fighting the fast ball off the other way. I want to do this for myself. I want to prove I *can* do it. But also, if I can hit different this year than I did last, it's going to throw the other teams off. It would start a gigantic circle of adjustments. A

pitcher can force me to adjust, but I always want to get into a position where I force him. Then I have the edge. Other teams know I'm a good low-ball, fast-ball hitter. A pitcher won't give me a fast ball, low and inside, but he might give me a fast ball up and in. When I'm working out, I ask our pitchers to give me the kind of balls I want to learn to hit.

Confidence has so much to do with a hitter. Confidence is a frame of mind. In baseball, your mind can be your best friend or your worst enemy. If you're in a slump, you can break and give in. I have photographs taken when I'm batting well and then when I'm batting badly. I can analyze and correct myself. I watch. I go back to fundamentals. I may be leading too much with my hips or my shoulders are dropping or my hands are not leading right. Many players only allow the team photographer to take pictures when they're in a slump. They have no comparisons to make. Pictures of me batting good help me to bat good again.

Some guys on the team have so much ability it's unbelievable. But when they hear the crowd in the stadium and feel the excitement, something happens. Like stage fright. I am sure some actors are outstanding in rehearsals, but when you open the curtain and there's people out there, they fall apart. When I get into the on-deck circle, I close out the stands. I start visualizing what I want to do. I start taking pictures of things I anticipate pitchers doing to me. In developing these pictures, I find myself executing different hits. My wife can't believe I don't hear her cheering when I'm up at bat, but I don't hear anything. I *see* myself hitting, even when I strike out! You have to create a frame of mind when you go to bat.

Good pitching always stops good hitting, but I have to say I'm better than the pitcher. The pitcher always says he is better than the batter. Gibson [Cardinals] and I have a battle going, like two boulders grinding against each other. Pitcher against batter is the greatest confrontation in sports.

Today you find more twenty-game winners among the pitchers, but I don't think the game has gone to the pitchers, because you find more .300 batters too. Some days a good pitcher is going to get you out and other days you'll hit him. You have to learn to defend yourself. That is partly a practical problem. After you have played ball for a while, you know how a pitcher throws and what he likes to throw. You know that when men are on base, the pitcher is going to throw a different way. Experience teaches you to measure these possibilities.

The pitcher–batter duel is also mental. You must tell yourself that the pitcher is not better than you. He's trying to get you out, but you are going to get a hit. If I am confident and in focus, I have a much better chance of hitting any kind of pitch out of the park.

A game that is on the line is a challenge to me. When we have a ten-run lead, I relax and don't concentrate as much. If the team needs my hit to win,

*Stargell works out with Dock Ellis*

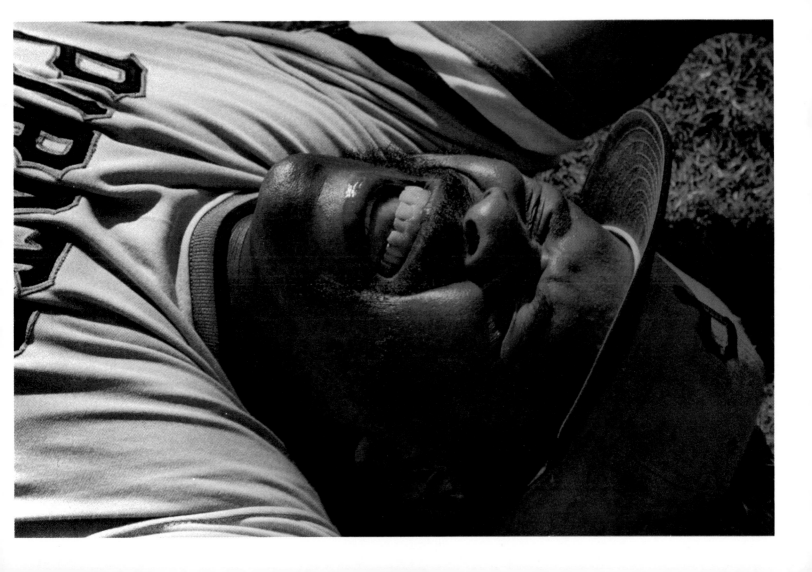

I get excited and tense. I can use those feelings to focus. There's just me at the plate. It is between the ball and me. I don't know what the outcome will be, but I can motivate myself to one-hundred-percent total concentration. If I do hit, I am personally satisfied. If I don't, I have to figure out why for myself—and that is not as easy as you might think. Baseball is a game of inches. You hit the ball just a quarter of an inch off center and it turns into a weak ground ball rather than a hard ground ball. I have to figure why I misjudged that fraction of an inch.

Training is putting the ingredients in the cake. Once you put the ingredients in, you can just about put the oven at the right temperature, and you'll be okay. You work like a dog in spring training to get into the groove and then you work to maintain that groove.

You have to shape up for endurance. After a number of years, you know what you need in training. The coach may say, "Run seven sprints," you know you need ten. You do ten. Whatever you put in is what you get out.

My legs are in pretty good shape now. My hands are beginning to callous. At first they bleed and I get blisters and bursts. Then they harden and I'm getting in shape.

This spring I have to work on my fielding. I had an operation on my knees in 1971 and management felt first base was the best place for me. Now I am permanent first baseman. I'll be working on ground balls and throwing bases. Charging bunts and making quick throws. A left-hander has an advantage at first. I can get the ball and throw directly to third, whereas the right-hander has to wheel around and lose time. When I get myself in register with the short throws, I won't have to think, "How'm I going to throw this ball?" I have got to get my first-baseman's instrument plugged in, because I am not going to be the player who hits home runs and then lets in fifteen or twenty runs with my glove.

As a team in spring training, you reacquaint youself with situations so you don't have to think. Great plays take care of themselves, but fundamentals, like catching ground balls, you have to master. We try to get a guy out quick. When the ball is hit, if it needs charging, we charge it. When we catch the ball, we get rid of it. When nobody is on base, we play the infield deeper. That way when a ground ball is hit deep, we can get the out.

Little things count. Take a game situation where there are men on first and third. Our object is to get that guy going home from third soon enough so we can also get the guy who is trying to go from second to third. We'll let him get past second and then nail him. If you can do these basics and score runs, you've got a pretty good team.

When we are doing well, we have a crazy bunch of guys. In 1966, we almost won the pennant. I remember marching around the clubhouse in World War I headgear with funny signs. We called ourselves the Black Maxers after an aviation film, *The Blue Max*. Stories were going around about the Green Weenie. Back before I joined the team, a Pirate trainer had noticed that whenever he pointed a green weenie at the opposing pitcher, the Pirates got a hit. The Green Weenie was just a big plastic frankfurter painted green, but it seemed to be magic. The fans caught on to Green Weenies in 1966. Whenever we needed a run for our side or our pitchers needed strikeouts, the fans would point those Weenies at the other team. A lot of players are superstitious and take those signs seriously. For me, it was fun. Baseball was a game again, played for its own sake.

In ball, so many things have no reason that you can see. I refuse to get spooked. I always try to find causes. I won't even get attached to my equipment. If I hit a long ball with one bat, I don't have to use that bat the next time up. If I were to lose a glove today, I'd go out and buy one and it would take me a day to break it in. I'd put my hand in it and then put it in the whirlpool. Water's about a hundred ten, a hundred twenty degrees. Then I take it out and beat it to the form of my hand. I hang it out with the heel down to dry. If it is a nice day, it will dry in about three hours. I put my hand back in and the glove is form fitting. I put baby oil up the crease and play catch to get me a pocket. It's used. There is no mystery to my gloves!

To some of the players, Clemente's death seems like an omen for this season. I know that baseball goes on with or without individuals. Clemente could have retired last year, or he could have been traded. In this game, you get used to meeting and getting to like guys and then they are no longer around, because they've been traded. But you can still meet up with them and talk with them. Roberto—it's the goodness in that man that I miss.

Sometimes I think this spring training will be my last one. Then I tell myself if I'm going to concentrate in the negative direction, I should give myself a chance to think positively. So I go out and work hard. If this is my last season, I can at least look back and say I tried my hardest.

It took time for me to feel this way. I used to think, "What am I doing wrong?" I was so wrapped up in what other people said that I really couldn't find out what was best for me. When I stopped thinking about outside comments, I could really concentrate on my performance. Life went on and I could sit down and talk to myself. "Who is suffering, me or them? I'm the one who has to deal with my problems." I'm not perfect, by no means, but I'm always learning. I'm not completely successful, but I'm growing.

Pride in your performance is the only important thing when you are out on the field. Money has nothing to do with it. It's a love of the game. When negotiations is over, you don't even think about dollars. All you really want to do is prove yourself year after year. Performance is more than ability. I've seen many guys with outstanding ability, but from a mental standpoint, they couldn't cope, and on Saturdays, they're at home watching us on TV. You have to have confidence and sacrifice.

# Stargell and Richie Hebner

*Rich:* You hit next Willie? I wouldn't mind hitting off this lefty, you know?

*Willie:* You want it?

*Rich:* How much milk you drink a day for power?

*Willie:* You hit me in the back six times!

*Rich:* How're you feeling, tiger?

*Willie:* We got three minutes to hit.

*Rich:* Put that bat down. (Referring to Willie's punches) Oh . . . (gets it in the gut)

*Willie:* You big bully! (Rich is now on the ground and Willie is laughing)

*Rich:* (begging) Willie, count to ten quick. I got to get to the field.

*Willie:* I didn't have to hit three minutes . . . you were down in two.

*Mrs. Clemente receives her husband's uniform*

# Opening Day

**Opening day in Pittsburgh featured
ceremonies honoring the late Roberto
Clemente. The Pirates then defeated the
St. Louis Cardinals in the ninth inning.**

Willie: Being behind in a game like today, you feel there is no way to come back, and then we do. We put a little fear in their hearts. It's psychologically good to know we can still do what we have done in the past.

Last year, we were behind in forty-two of the games we won. I've had friends leave the stadium in the bottom of the eighth and feel bad because we were losing. They would hear a roar while they were driving home, turn on the radio and find out we had won again. Personally, I hate to lose. I try to win, even at tiddlywinks.

Everyone is sad this year about the loss of Roberto Clemente. He was a great hitter. He was a great fielder. But we will miss him most as a man. During spring training, the team was watching to see if I would play a different role because Roberto was gone. People be saying I'm going to pick up the slack in leadership, but there is no role I'm going to perform. I'm not looking for a job. Some guys are sensitive because of what has been said about me being the new leader. But guys who really know me, they know I'm not going to change.

This is the best shape I have ever been in. It's the first spring training I have completed in good health. Even my legs are feeling good. I've passed the endurance test. After the morning workout, I played nine innings every day and then did additional running. I used to be good for nothing at the end of the day, but this year I went home and played with the kids without being completely fatigued. I plan to stay healthy all year. My goal is to hit fifty home runs and drive in one hundred sixty. I want an outstanding year.

Now I have been switched back to left field. I'm worried about throwing long, because at first base I worked all spring to shorten my throw. I discussed the move back to left with Virdon. First of all, Robertson had a real great spring, hitting and fielding. After his bad year, he deserves another shot. Year before last he hit twenty-six home runs.

I am concerned that we win and I don't feel I'm putting my job in jeopardy by going to left field. If I felt my legs couldn't do it, I would be embarrassed for myself and the ballclub. Last year I had problems, because my knee hadn't healed. The doctors were telling me it was going to get better, but I felt that it wasn't. Because of my knees, I thought I would have to play first base, whether I played that position for the Pirates or not.

My wheels are okay now. I'm going to wear greyhound shoes. They have a plastic bottom that doesn't hold the heat as much as rubber. They're good for traction when you are traveling in excess of the speed limit, like I do!

**In the locker room after winning against
St. Louis on opening day.**

Stargell finishes an interview with a reporter in his official voice: "Winning the first game adds to your motivation and confidence."

Meanwhile in the clubhouse, a white player ribs his black teammate,

"Hey, gar."

"Gar who?"

"Nig-gar."

"Some joke!"

An infielder peers over an outfielder's shoulder. "That wouldn't be a phone number, would it?"

"Get the fuck out of here."

"You're sure my friend. We requested lockers next to each other, and if I had a roommate on the road, it would be you."

"Cut that shit out now."

"I heard about those broads you be fucking at the motel. One of them got a wig. A nice wig. When she runs the bases with you, it falls off!"

"Don't you know Sally's going to slap the shit out of you for fooling around with those girls."

"There you go. Playing violin music. But I'll give you Joy's number."

"I remember when you used to leave tickets for all those fucking broads. But after you got married, you did quit."

"I still leave tickets for a girl named Merry Christmas."

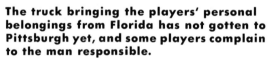

**The truck bringing the players' personal
belongings from Florida has not gotten to
Pittsburgh yet, and some players complain
to the man responsible.**

"Hey, where is the fucking truck?"

"I have some kids crying at home because they haven't got no bicycles."

"I have blankets on the truck and I'm freezing. It's still winter here."

"My fucking fire is on the truck. You'd better get it here or my hands won't be warm enough to pitch."

The man says, "Oh, come off it guys. The truck's coming."

One player is ready to leave and asks, "How's the mob outside?"

"Bad. It's going to be bad for a half an hour getting out of here. It's a real bitch when it gets jammed up."

An infielder is shaving. Someone teases, "Hey, whatcha doing, shaving now? You're supposed to shave before the shower. Is that the way Italians do it? Get better shaves after the shower?"

"Only niggers do it before."

"What time we supposed to be here tomorrow?"

"We have workout at eleven."

*Poster in the locker room*

**Toward the end of the first month of the season, the Pirates have a losing record. Five games have been canceled by either rain or freezing weather.**

Willie: I'm back to normal again in the outfield. It was strange for the first couple of games, being there in the wide, open spaces. When you don't play a position for a long time, you have to reacquaint yourself. Spring training is the time to start again, but this year, April has been my training month.

We haven't started as a contending team should. Guys are coming to the ball park not knowing what position they are going to play, or even if they are going to play at all. Trouble is, Bill Virdon has to answer for his moves. He is questioned, because he is new. When moves don't work, the players say Virdon is wrong. Murtaugh juggled the team around too, but he did it in a different way. He knew how to treat men.

Coming out of spring training, Murtaugh used to say, "That's your job and the only person can take it away or lose it will be you." If you fucked up, he'd call you in and say, "Hey, you're not doing the job for me. I gotta get somebody else in there. I'm just gonna give you a little rest. I am pretty sure that's all you need. Go out there and get your running and hitting in and I'll get you back into the lineup."

Instead of sitting in a corner, you'd get your head together and work on your problems. With Murtaugh, you were always ready to respond if you were called upon. Murtaugh was an experienced manager and Bill Virdon isn't. He just started last year.

I think Bill does a hell of a job, but Danny Murtaugh gave the team more confidence. Bill tells a guy the truth, but most guys don't want to be told that they are playing bad. So under Virdon, the team is pulling apart. If Bill takes a guy out, he mopes. If a guy isn't called upon to pinch-hit, he drags. If a guy is called on to pinch-hit and he'd rather be playing, he shows he is pissed off by not hitting. We are not a team.

When we are working as a unit, one guy fucks up and someone comes to his aid. An infielder makes an error and the pitcher makes an extra effort to make sure he don't allow a base hit. Now everybody knows they have a job to do, but they won't push little petty jealousies aside. We have a lot of unhappy guys on the Pirates. This ballclub is a disturbed place.

If we were winning, we would all feel like playing a complete game —offensively and defensively. It's more of a grind since we're losing. I can remember times when the Pirates were down and I dreaded going to the ballpark. We haven't gotten to that point yet, but we're close.

I still have confidence in myself no matter what. I am going to have a good year. I play tricks with my mind. I try and make a habit of telling myself that no one is going to get me out at the plate. I'm not foolish enough to think I am going to go the whole year without striking out, but that's what I keep telling myself. If my mind is going to play tricks, they're going to be positive tricks. That is mental control.

I just feel I'm going to hit. I try not to be anxious, because I will get too excited. I calm myself by twirling the bat. I also twirl the bat because, if I stand there waiting for the pitcher to pitch, I tend to lock the muscles in my forearms, wrists, and hands. Then I can't swing. Twirling slows my bat down and enables me to hit properly. That's probably the only way I can hit.

I wait for a pitch that is in my zone, waist high, right over the plate. That's the pitch I have been best with over the years.

I am a power hitter. I have the full swing. I would rather strike out than have a controlled swing. To maintain my swing through the entire season, I am going to be off judgment sometimes, because I have to commit myself quicker than most guys. When Oliver hits, he stands and waits and waits and waits. Then he may pass a pitch up. But Oliver hits the ball more than I do. He makes more contact. I could change my swing and go for an average, but I don't try to be a different hitter than I am.

When I find a bat that is comfortable, I use it all season. Once I did a little drilling, which is illegal. Everyone was throwing spitballs and I said, "I'm going to put some cork in my bat." That is how I retaliated. I hit a ball that went unbelievably out of center field in San Francisco. Then one day a guy pitched me inside and broke the bat. I could see the cork fly, but no one else did. If they had, I would have been fined.

Pitchers make me mad when they are not giving me good pitches. When they don't want me to hurt them with the long ball, they pitch me different. Rather than throw a ball knee-high, they'll throw it low to bait me. If I take the bait, then nine times out of ten, I'm not successful. They know I'll bite for the low pitch, because I can't resist trying. I'm not as cool as Stan Musial. I just love to swing.

Pitchers shouldn't let a hot hitter beat them unless that hitter's got someone behind him that's just as hot. We have such a powerful lineup that the opposing pitchers don't have much choice. If they walk me, they get to Hebner and he can do bad damage.

The only power in our lineup that has been having problems is Robertson. I have told him that he lifts his shoulder when he swings, but he's thinking about everything else and confusing himself. Slumps are designed to see how long an individual is going to stay in one. They are mental. A guy may have only one thing to correct, but his mind starts telling him, "I'm in a slump. My hands aren't working. I'm opening up my body too quick for my hands." If you are thinking about what your hands do or where your body is, the ball goes right past you. Rather than missing the ball for a week or two at the most, you stay in a slump for a month. That's what happens to Robertson. He gets really messed up by thinking too much and he can't hit.

We have an unusual ballclub. Most of the guys are young and unseasoned. They can't deal with losing. They have never been on a losing ballclub. No play is a matter of life and death. One player thinks if he doesn't perform, someone else will. Guys go out and do a half-assed job. Players say, "I don't feel good today, so I'll just go through the motions and let somebody else do it." You can't win that way. Our team is not giving one hundred percent. That's not good.

When you lose, which we have been doing, if you've gone out and given your best, you don't break. That's how I keep going. I can bend without breaking. In the minor leagues, I had four years of frustration. I wanted to do good, but when I was going bad, I let it affect me for weeks. Now if I make an error, it stays with me in the outfield. I don't bring it to the plate. I drop it. Physical mistakes I'm going to make. I am going to drop balls. When you have to look right into the sun, there's no way on earth you can catch every ball. I do try to limit my mental mistakes—like making a throw to the wrong base. That shows lack of concentration and makes me real mad at myself. I have to keep mental control.

Baseball comes down to how well an individual is doing. When the ball is hit to you in the outfield or the infield, it's a one-to-one situation. You and the ball. If you had a good break on the fly ball in the infield, but the ball drops dead, you can't go and make excuses. You could cry to other players and newspapermen, but you're going to have to live with yourself. *You* know what happened.

Deep down I feel that when you have the bat in your hands and don't hit, when you get the glove in your hand and you don't catch, regardless of what people say, you're the one has that strange feeling inside.

I've been on the club longer than anybody. If I go up and start telling people how I handle different feelings, some guys will say, "He's trying to be leader." They'll resent me. If guys come to me, I talk to them. I've talked to Clines all season. He wanted to be traded, because he has felt discriminated against. He didn't even have a chance to try out for right field in spring training. They just gave it to Manny so they could have the Great White Hope behind the plate. The Pirates are afraid to field an all black team. They don't put the nine best men on the field, because of the fans. Young boy comes to the stadium and identifies with the ballplayers. Don't matter to him if they are black or blue. But it matters to his father. He don't want that son worshiping a black man. And it's even worse when the sixteen-year-old daughter starts mooning over some black man!

**In New York on May 18 the Pirates dropped a Friday-night game to the Mets, but have come back on Saturday afternoon to defeat the Mets with a tenth-inning homer by Stargell.**

Willie:    No question about it. If Robertson hadn't hit the home run in the ninth today, we wouldn't have been in the ball game. He just set it up for me. A home run always breaks up a game. Even for the guy that's pitching an outstanding game—boom, there is the home run. The big spoil. Base running and the guy with speed is exciting, but the most damaging thing in baseball is the long ball.

I was impressed with the way Matlack [the Mets' pitcher] came back today. The next-to-last time up, he threw me a slider and I hit the ball real good, but Harrelson made an even better catch. I'd like to have gotten a hit, because we would have gotten a run. But when you are in the major leagues, you're playing against top ballplayers; Harrelson made an outstanding play and the out was made. I was mad for a minute, but I didn't allow myself to dwell on it. Like, tomorrow I can't feel great about my home run today. I still have a job to do, and I have to do it every game.

One manager I played for platooned me, but I have never allowed myself to think I could not be a complete ballplayer against either right-handers or left-handers. I got to the major leagues by hitting everybody. If you can hit, you can hit anybody. If you're not hitting, you won't hit left- or right-handers. I have been in slumps where I faced five or six right-handers and didn't hit them. I don't believe in platooning, even though it is true that I can see the ball a lot longer against right-handers.

I haven't been hitting the ball that well in the last five or six ball games, but I have to keep grinding. The first part of the year I enjoyed a great start, then I trailed off and wasn't driving in runs. I knew it was just a matter of time before I could get a good, consistent stroke. Hitting is such a mystery. Some days I come to the ballpark and feel exceptionally well physically and mentally and I don't do a thing. Days when I feel tired, I have my greatest day. You can't take anything for granted in baseball.

I thought Nellie [Briles] pitched a tremendous ballgame against Matlack today. Seems like the other team can't get any runs when he pitch. Dave [Giusti] came in and did a tremendous job. So did Ramon Hernandez. Relief pitching is tough, but they are exceptional people. Turn the light green and they get out of a difficult spot. Come in, throw strikes, and get the guy out.

Last night, although we lost to Seaver, we kept the game close. That meant something to us as a team, because we have never to this point given up on ourselves. We feel that we are a good ballclub and just haven't indicated it yet. We need some coordination. We lost last night, but we won

today. We're never going to give up on ourselves no matter what.

People say we are losing, because we have lost our leader. There will never be another Clemente, but we realize that if he were here when we are down, he would say: You gotta go out there and play good ball. That's what you owe yourself and your fans.

I believe in a team working together as equals. Leadership is one person dictating to another person who takes orders. We're all professionals. We know the job we have to do. We don't need one guy to keep telling us.

Right now I'm just physically down. I feel like I've been in a hatchet fight and everybody had a hatchet but me. I feel like I've been over ninety miles of bad road. I am exhausted.

I was glad to see Maury Wills today. He is definitely qualified to manage in the major leagues. There are many blacks qualified in this business. All we have to do is hire them! I've always wondered: Is it color they hate? Is it a social standard where if you're not part of a group, then you're an outcast? I talk about race more than I used to. My feelings are seeping out little by little. I used to be so upset that I kept it all inside.

I remember one particular day in the minors we were in Hobbs, New Mexico, where they had a special section for blacks. One inning I was coming from first base to the dugout and I heard a couple of blacks say, "That's a skinny, no-good nigger." That really hurt me. We had another black player who came from the South in the middle of the season whose name was Mason. Rather than go in the dugout and talk, I called him outside. We were hitting an inning and the manager, who was coaching third base, saw us talking outside the dugout. He thought we were out there bullshitting. When the game was over, he said we weren't interested in playing and if he had his way, he would get some ballplayers who cared. I told him why we were talking, how I felt bad about being called nigger by another black. It must have touched him, because he said he was sorry. I said, "When there's a question concerning me, just ask me first and I'll give you first-hand information." I have always dealt man to man.

Race hit me like a ton of bricks when I got into minor-league professional ball. Before that I had lived in integrated projects. Some of my best friends in grade school were Chinese, Mexican, and white guys. I fell in love with a redheaded, freckle-face girl. Discrimination hit me in 1959 on my way to play my first year of professional ball. I left San Francisco with three other guys at twelve midnight and we flew all night and all day to this town called Jackson. I had no idea where we were! On the flight, the only things they gave us was hot chocolate. I was young and had quite an appetite, so when we saw a sign at the airport that said Restaurant, the four of us headed for it. This man jumped up from the cashier's desk and said, "Hey, you niggers. Get out of here. You know we can't serve you." It was a cold, eerie feeling that went over me, but the other two guys who were white said, "If you can't eat here, then we're not going to."

We were walking out the door and a black redcap said, "Son, don't you know where you are?" I said no. He said, "You're in Mississippi. Jackson, Mississippi. You can't eat in those places with those white people. You have to go around back." Black people in the South have learned their place.

We were still hungry, so we proceeded to go around back. There was a partioned area and you had to fight flies with one hand and ants with the other. They had a little bench and tables made of cheap wood. Somebody said, "Hey, what do you want?" But I had lost my appetite.

When we got to Jacksonville, we took a bus to Jacksonville Beach. The white guys stayed on the beach and we stayed in a place called Black Bottom. It was a big, empty house with ten or twelve army cots lined up against the wall. I didn't appreciate the roaches and rats, but I either had to stay there or up over the 600 Club. Later I stayed over the club, which was in a black section of town. My room was up over the jukebox. I can remember word for word, beat for beat, one song they played all night and day: "Go, Go, Little Queenie" by Chuck Berry. People danced on cement floors with sand on them and I had to adapt to this tempo in order to sleep.

During my first year in the minors, my monthly salary was a hundred seventy-five dollars; the next year it jumped to two fifty-five! They gave us meal tickets for breakfast and dinner which were like Fort Knox in your hand, because if you lost those tickets, you didn't eat. The breakfast ticket entitled you to eggs, grits, and a form of meat. We would all go to a restaurant on the bus, but the white guys would go inside where it was air-conditioned. The blacks would go in the back behind the kitchen in a little shack with no windows, just a squeaking door, long tables, and benches. Black guys who worked in the kitchen would pile plates on top of trays and bring them out the back door where all the garbage cans and flies were. When they got to the door of the shack where we were, we'd fight for the food like POWs. Guys with seniority would get their food first.

If you wanted to splurge and get fried chicken, hush puppies, and mashed potatoes, you'd have to take your breakfast ticket and put it with your dinner ticket. But if you did that, the only food you'd get for the rest of the day would be a sandwich and some pop at the ballpark.

A friend of mine called Feets came through from California. I only had five or six dollars, because payday was ten days off. We bought a dozen eggs and five pounds of potatoes and a pound or two of onions and cooked all this together in a big old pot. I was staying in a rented room in a private home. I could use the refrigerator, so I put this big old pot in the refrigerator and scooped out segments every day. They were pretty good meals, but they wasn't enough. We got the flies off and then scrapped over the food. Flies made it so uncomfortable. Besides it was blistering hot. We knew other players were sitting in a nice, comfortable, white restaurant with air-conditioning. This was spring training, where we stayed for six weeks. After that, they gave us money for a bus from Jacksonville Beach, Florida, to San Angelo, Texas. It seemed like a week we traveled on that bus.

We were drawing so poorly in San Angelo that they had to switch the franchise to Roswell, New Mexico. I mean that was poor. We played other minor-league teams from major-league affiliates. Like Midland, Texas, was a Milwaukee Braves ball club. When we played in Artesia, New Mexico, a San Francisco Giants club, I could only get accommodations at a lady's home. She raised baits for fishing—worms and night crawlers—but she raised them inside. You couldn't believe the odor. No air-conditioning. And she nailed her windows down, so we had to sleep with this odor. If you wanted to eat, you had to go downtown to the back of a restaurant. They would throw a napkin down on huge meat-chopping blocks with flies, blood stains, and bits of meat. Charged the same prices that they did out front. Rather than eat there, I would go to a store to buy meat, sardines or sausages, cream-puff pies, pop, and milk. This is how I made my meal.

Playing ball in Texas, they would harass the hell out of me and call me everything but a child of God. I was so saddened, I wouldn't even concentrate. I had no desire. As a matter of fact, I used to hate to go to the ballpark, because people singled out the blacks. They would use "nigger" in so many different terms—"pork chops" and "black Puerto Ricans." It got so bad I used to cry myself to sleep at night. There were only two other blacks—one was from Cuba and the other from the Dominican Republic. They couldn't speak English and I couldn't speak Spanish. Only thing I could do was call home every once in a while and get some reassurance. My parents would tell me I could come home, but I wanted to play ball so bad that I stayed in Texas.

I still haven't been able to find out all these years what it is that makes people prejudiced? Take blind people who don't know what color a person is. If their head is together, then there's a sense of communication. I'll be talking to people and mention someone's name. First thing they say, "What color is he? Black? Or what?"

Funny thing is I don't give a fuck what color you are, you can damn near demand respect, or command it if you got the money. It's that fucking green Jesus. If you're happy, then money don't mean a damn thing. The green Jesus. That's what it is. That's what everybody praises. You can kill your mama, get a good lawyer, plead insanity, and beat it every time. You go to the bank to steal a dollar and you've got good sense. If you are after money, society approves and understands you.

**Willie returns to his suite in the Essex House in New York to relax for the evening. He returns a few phone calls.**

Willie: Hello, is this Angela? I'm fine. How you doing? You sound like a million dollars. I was surprised when I saw this message that I could call any time. Sure good hearing your voice . . . Oh, Dock's fine. He's going to pitch in Philadelphia. Yeah, we're going there tomorrow after the game and we play Monday night, Tuesday, and Wednesday. See you later tonight? Okay.

Willie: I used to think that women just come with the game. In the minors, it wasn't easy. Guys didn't have much money and they'd just blow through towns and get bad reputations. But once you play in the majors, there are more women than you can handle. Come back to your room after the game and there's messages from Sheila, Pat, and I don't know who.

In the beginning, I was fascinated, but a lot of things happened. I got two women pregnant in 1962. I liked both of them to a certain degree, but I didn't want to get married. I still felt I had to do the right thing, so I got tied up with the woman I had known the longest. After that was over, I began to be picky about the women I saw. I like to get together with someone, because it breaks up the monotony of road trips and you can slowly unwind after a game. I need the relaxation.

My old lady may assume I'm screwing around, but she doesn't know that I do. I have always felt that no one should know everything about a person. It's not a matter of what's right and wrong. But if life at home is smooth, that's better for me. I do know that if my wife fooled around while I was on the road, I would kill her!

**Willie and his wife Dee reminisce in a
restaurant after a game.**

Dee: Remember when I didn't know what baseball was? When we met in the bathroom after you came into the ladies' room by mistake?

Willie: No . . . we met after a fashion show that night.

Dee: I was modeling then, but I wasn't in that show. You caught my eyes.

Willie: *You* cursed me out.

Dee: I just got mad at you, because you were talking to one of the girls in the show for half the night. After she left, you came over and asked for my number. I said it was none of your damned business.

Willie: The ironic thing was the next day . . .

Dee: A week later . . .

Willie: . . . I went to the hospital for an operation and I'd just come out from the anesthetic, and there you was, walking through the door. I figured you must have the wrong room.

Dee: I figured I was nasty to you, but I was just mad, because you were talking to that other girl.

Willie: I wasn't talking to her.

Dee: You were with her all night!

Willie: [*Obviously repeating an old argument*] No, we were dancing, because she was from Haiti and I had just returned from the Dominican Republic. She danced the way they danced!

Dee: But you danced all night.

Willie: I was a real freak for dancing. I didn't talk though. We were dancing fast and didn't have time for no talking.

Dee: You were talking . . .

Willie: [*Kidding*] Just moving fast.

Dee: I'll never forget it.

Willie: For seven years, you haven't forgotten. Chances are you won't.

Dee: I think you went there to be with her afterwards. . .

Willie: That *was* a very exciting evening.

Dee: Then I saw in the papers you were in the hospital and I realized who you were. I asked you what kind of bread you bought. [*laughs*] I thought famous people ate different bread. I always thought there were special stores for famous people!

Willie: When I borrowed some money from you because I was broke, fast, all the fantasy wore off.

**Dee Stargell, at home in Pittsburgh, discusses her life with Willie while he is on a road trip.**

Dee: I was awfully depressed this week. I felt so down. I sit here not wanting for anything and being happy in my marriage. My children are not sickly, but I don't have any more friends. I feel kind of weird.

When I married Willie, I was just thinking about the glamorous life I was going to have. I didn't think there'd be any problems. It looks so different from the outside world.

People do show you special attention. When I buy something in a store and give them my credit card, they say, "Oh, Mrs. *Stargell*." At first, I adored it. I would come in and there'd be ten people waiting on line and they would take *me*. I was thrilled.

I wasn't as bad as Dave Cash's wife. She thought everyone would suddenly recognize her when she married Cash. The guys at the ticket window don't know who you are right away. They would ask her name and she'd say, all insulted, "I'm Mrs. Cash." Snotty. She expected everyone to fall at her feet. The guards used to stop her and say, "You can't go through this entrance. It's for the players' wives." She'd say, "Well, don't you know who I am!"

I was disappointed in another way. I didn't miss the glamour. After I found out that Willie used the same kind of toothpaste I did, I knew that ballplayers were human. It was no big deal. But I somehow thought that Willie would be home every day. I didn't want him on the road. We were engaged for about a year. When he went away, it seemed awful long then.

I don't feel as insecure now as I used to. When I first met Willie, he was just getting divorced. The girl was a showy type. She wasn't that good-looking, but she loved to get dressed up, go out, and spend money. Of course, Willie does too. He's ridiculous. He goes out and buys expensive clothes in weird velvet and silk. Then they go out of style and he throws them out after he's flashed once. All the ballplayers buy expensive toys like BB guns and hundred-dollar fishing rods. It looks like they're just throwing money away. I guess they never had it, so now they buy whatever they want to.

Willie left his first wife alone all the time. He'd go to play winter ball in the Dominican Republic and she would stay in California. Finally they went to a marriage counselor and the guy said, "I'm supposed to get people back together and I've never recommended anyone going apart, but I think you two should get a divorce." It must have been pretty bad. That's about the time I met Willie and he said he would never get married again.

I'd been going out with another black ballplayer—Don Clendenon. He went on to play for New York and now he is out of ball. I didn't really like him that much, but we had fun. When I met Willie, I just told Don I'd met someone I liked better. Clendenon found out it was Willie and used to tease him on the bench and call him backstabber. He never did like Willie anyway. They were both big hitters.

I was just another one of Willie's victims. I got pregnant too. Then we decided to get married. I was making preparations and all of a sudden, Willie changed his mind. I was furious, but Willie didn't want to get married. I didn't want to put pressure on him, even though I was pregnant. He went back to California and finally he called me to come out. I never knew whether Willie really liked me or just felt sorry for me. Of course, there's lots of women he's gotten pregnant that he didn't marry so maybe he did like me. But I've always felt very insecure about that.

Willie is basically a good person. He might have married me out of the kindness of his heart. I worried since he rejected me just before we were supposed to get married. But I'll tell you, when he called from California, I caught the first flight out of Pittsburgh to get hooked up.

We stayed in California until February, when he was going to spring training. I came home, lived with my mother and started looking for an apartment in Pittsburgh. I'd call up from an ad and they would tell me to come out to look at the apartment. When I'd get there, they had just rented that apartment, but they still wanted Willie's autograph. You can't tell from the name Stargell whether someone's black or white. They knew Willie was a ballplayer, who had just come up from the minors, but they didn't know what color he was. This happened in so many places that I was getting dejected. I was driving around in my mother's little car. It wouldn't start half the time. I was pregnant and getting tired of looking.

One morning, I read about a place that sounded pretty nice. I called and said I was Mrs. Stargell and I was black. If the apartment had already been rented to let me know now, because I wasn't going all the way out there so she should tell me the place had been rented and could she please have an autographed picture. The woman said come out and I took the apartment that day. She didn't even know who Willie was.

In 1968 I was the only black ballplayer's wife. I didn't have any friends to talk with or to relate my experiences to. It was a lonesome life, kind of miserable. I could go out and throw twenty dollars away on myself, but I didn't know anyone else who could afford to do what I liked. It's probably like having an old girlfriend, somebody you made mud pies with. If you met that friend later on and you were Mrs. Nixon and she was just where she was the last time you saw her—making mud pies and on welfare—just making it from day to day, naturally you wouldn't be as close as you were.

I found myself alone with a lot of people around me. It was like being alone in New York with six million people. Nobody had anything in common with me. I was making more money than anybody I knew, or my husband was, and I was actually apprehensive about making friends. I didn't trust anybody. I couldn't get close to a soul.

I don't think other ballplayers' wives particularly like me anyway. It's a funny feeling I have. I don't feel real comfortable with them. I think they should understand me. We're all in the same situation, but they seem to resent Willie's position with the club, so they automatically resent me. They feel jealousy. They know that Willie makes more than their husbands.

I have other interests than the wives. I don't know exactly how they spend their time. Going crazy, I guess. Sometimes they play cards. I try and read, but I don't read as much as I should. I'm so doggone busy doing nothing that I don't have time to sit with the girls. I just feel strange around them.

One time we had a little meeting with all the wives. I tried to be friendly with everybody. There was gossip and I tried to make some cracks to stop that kind of talk—about women on the road and the possibility of our going on the road. I could go on the road now—if I wanted to pay a fine every time I'm caught. We're not allowed to travel. It's a two-hundred-fifty-dollar fine the first time we're caught in the same city where the guys are playing. It's weird. This is just a Pirates' rule and I don't think it's fair. We're old enough to make up our own minds. Actually, the guys play better when they are home than they do on the road, so the team can't argue that wives are bad for them. My personal opinion is that the guys raise so much hell on the road, it's better if the wives don't go.

Of course, we all get real skeptical about our husbands being away. I guess I trust Willie enough. I used to worry in the beginning, but then I made myself stop. You can't worry about things you don't know definitely about, even though you've got a strong suspicion. I always thought the main problem of being married to a ballplayer would be other women—flirting with them and all that. Men do it anyway, but because Willie's a ballplayer, he gets more action than the average guy. I accept that. When he starts treating me different, then I'll worry about it.

I would rather have Willie fool around away from home in the summer months. At least he has someone to look forward to on the road. All the players probably have girls in the different cities they visit two or three times a year. If there's somebody in St. Louis who's content with seeing Willie three times a year and can be bothered with that kind of arrangement, then if it's okay with her, it's okay with me.

Willie and I have talked about women in a roundabout way. He'd tell me about this one ballplayer who had gotten hurt and came home early as a surprise. Found his wife in bed with another man. See, I know from Willie's schedule when he'll be here and when he won't. I could do anything I want while he's away. I've dreamed about it, but Willie said he would kill me if I ever did. I was still immature when I thought about other men. Willie and I have a good sex life, but it's not really enough. But now I'm so busy preaching the Gospel that I don't have time to think about sex!

Every now and then, Willie brings home a card from somebody who "misses" him "very much." Just funny little cards signed by women. Willie denies everything. As long as he denies it, that's fine with me. It can never hurt me if I don't know about it specifically. Sometimes I get mad. It depends on the mood I'm in. I can get suspicious and feel insecure. Especially when he's been gone a long time. I'll try to call a couple of nights in a row and he's never at the hotel. I wonder, "What the heck is he doing?" When he's in California, he has a good excuse. He can say he's been with one of his children or his mother or his sister. I've just stopped calling, because he's never there. Sure these are problems for me, but I can't see discussing them with the other wives. They are a private matter that is just between Willie and me.

Now we have more black wives on the team, but I'm not that close to them. In spring training, Donna Oliver told me that she couldn't figure me out. We were sitting around drinking wine and she said she was going home to figure me out. Next time I saw her, I asked if she had. I was laughing, because I didn't think she was serious. She said, "No, I still can't find out why we're not close."

Actually, Willie's changed lately too. He's not even as close to Dock Ellis as he used to be. Now we make arrangements to meet other ballplayers and they cancel out. I wouldn't make anything of it if it happened now and then, but it happens consistently, so there must be something to it. Other players' wives think I'm weird, because I'll say, "As long as I don't know what Willie's doing, let him have a ball." They say, "Are you serious?" "Do you really feel that way?" "I don't believe it." "It couldn't be. Never."

People will always think we have a glamorous life, but as wives we don't. We're not included in club events. They didn't want to let us on the team plane to Clemente's funeral. They couldn't believe that we cared too. As a player's wife, you lose your whole identity, your man, your everything. You don't even recognize your first name any more, because you're no longer Dolores, you're Willie's wife. That's your name.

I do have some advantages. Every winter we get six weeks in Florida while Willie's at spring training. It's a nice change for me after the cold winter. Willie doesn't like it though. It's day in and day out exercising. Work time. He's harder for me in Florida. I enjoy it, but he's so miserable I used to leave. When he came home for dinner one night, I was gone.

Once I rode down to spring training with Willie, but I didn't like that. I think he was mad to have me along, because he probably visits his old girlfriends on the road when I'm not there. Now he drives down for the first two weeks and I come when he's mentally and physically ready for the family! While I'm there, we have a house in Holmes Beach. Willie stays at the Holiday Inn when I'm not around. You're not supposed to stay off the Pirate City barracks unless your wife is there, but Willie rents our house to one of the coaches and sneaks into a motel.

Now during the season, when Willie's on the road, we talk once or twice a day. He tells me if he gets hurt or has a cold or if he's had a good game. Willie wants me to be concerned to the point where everything is fine and I watch the games, but not to the point where I think he might never hit another ball. When he goes into a really bad slump, I get worried. At first I shrug it off: "Think you'll get a hit today?"

He'll kid: "Routine. Routine." He usually makes a joke about it. If I start getting serious, he thinks I am worrying and he'll start worrying and get more upset. Besides, it seems like a private thing between Willie and baseball. I still try to help Willie when he's down. I'll tell him, "If you can't do it, then nobody else can." Or, "You're the only one that can get yourself out of this." Mostly I can tell his mood by the tone of his voice. He might say, "I don't think I'll ever play again." Then he's really depressed and I can tell. I know I'm not that much help, but when the Pirates are losing and Willie gets really difficult, I'll say, "You're not the only one on the team." We are more in touch when he is on the road than when he's home.

If the game is on TV, I watch with the children. They want to know why they can't go down to Three Rivers Stadium. I say, "Nobody's there. When the game's on TV, they're not in town." Son-son [the Stargell's six-year-old boy] is beginning to understand, but Kellie [their three-year-old girl], no. One day I'm going to take her down with the television set and put it in the middle of the empty field and watch the game.

When Willie's on the road for a long trip, the kids act up. They don't listen to me. I hate it, because my patience isn't that long for them. I get upset and call Willie; he'll talk to them and calm them down. Otherwise, I complain a lot, but they're no big problem. They wander around outside all day.

Son-son has been going to school since he was two. A two year old doesn't know much about what his father does. Some older kids would say, "That's Willie Stargell's son." He began to understand what that meant. Then kids started coming over to the house for autographs. When Son-son started playing in the father–son games, he would offer the fans *his* autograph.

We didn't want Son-son to be treated different, but people just do. When he was three, we asked his professor at this special school at the University of Pittsburgh whether young Willie knew what his father did. The Professor said that Son-son knew his father was something special.

At checkout counters in the grocery store, the lady will lean over and say, "What's your name, little boy?" Now Son-son says, "My name is Willie and my father's a famous baseball player." I hope Son-son will handle it.

Children have seemed to be an excuse for Willie to leave me behind at home. He was in Cincinnati when I had Kellie. She was a surprise too. I messed up with my birth-control pills. When I went to the doctor, I came out depressed: Oh, no, I'm pregnant again. I had a mental block, because Willie would make me stay locked up in the house with the kids. If I wanted to go out to dinner, Willie would say, "How can you leave the child with a babysitter? You've only known her for two weeks." He was all concerned about the baby and I felt neglected anyway. I hated the whole business of children and taking care of them.

I have also been turned off children because of my own family. I grew up with a lot of kids. It was always a food shortage and I could never get any new clothes. At school picnics, I wore hand-me-downs. When we were called for dinner, it was beans again tonight. I didn't enjoy coming up. I got depressed because I couldn't have the things I wanted. I always appreciated my mother going out and working in some white people's house. I knew that she didn't have to do it if it wasn't for us, but every year she got pregnant again. I couldn't stand it. I was third from the oldest and raised the younger children. When I was graduated from high school, my mother was forty and couldn't even attend graduation because she was in the hospital having another baby, her eleventh.

I never even thought about having kids until I met Willie. He was talking about how he wanted to have ten children. We had gone together for so long waiting on his divorce. I started thinking about a baby and then it happened. The marriage came finally.

Kids have been depressing for me. I would like to have one child that wasn't an accident, but now I feel that if I tried, I probably couldn't get pregnant, because I would want to. Also, Willie thinks I'm awful when I'm pregnant. I don't feel that bad, but Willie says my eighth and ninth months are terrible. Actually, if I'm going to have a child, I would have to get pregnant right away, because the world is going to end in 1975. I have a little time left, but it's now or never.

Willie may want a lot of kids, but he only likes being with the children more or less. He pretends to be so concerned when he can't be with the kids during the summer. I get up and take them to school when he's sleeping, and by the time they get back around three, he has gone to the ballpark. Then he doesn't see them again until they're asleep. If I didn't sleep with Willie, I would never see him either.

I used to feel part of everything Willie did. When he would fall or slide, it hurt me. I couldn't stand for anything to touch his leg or knee when they were giving him trouble. I used to say, "How's our knee?" "Don't be sliding on my knee." I never felt that I was part of the hit, but I do feel I am part of Willie. I feel I am part of his body.

One day I came to the stadium late as usual. Everybody was standing up. If someone had hit a home run, they would have been clapping. The stadium was quiet. Everybody was looking toward left field. I got on my knees and prayed. Finally I looked up over the crowd and there was Willie laying there in front of the scoreboard. It turned out that his teeth were bashed out and his lip all swollen. I flew down to the clubhouse. I was the first woman in that place.

The doctor was telling me, "Don't get panicky now when you see him." He was laying there, blinking his eyes. "I'm okay, honey."

I said, "Oh, sure you are. You look terrible." I always try not to show my concern, because he gets upset when I worry. In many ways, Willie treats me like a child. He doesn't think I can handle any problems, so I don't hear them. After that accident, Willie started getting headaches. I thought his career was over, but I never told him. One day, he snapped out of the headaches and had a future again.

Willie and I talk about the club sometimes. Willie has told me that Scoop [Al Oliver] is the best first baseman in the National League, but the front office had him moved over to center field so Robertson, who is white, can play first base. Joe Brown runs the whole show—the front office, the field—everything comes from him. Willie is convinced of this anyway. The club is like a puppet show with Brown pulling the strings. He understands what he wants to understand.

I think management discriminates against the black players on the team. The Latin players are just grateful to be in the United States making forty thousand dollars a year. They would never make that kind of money in Puerto Rico. The black players used to be grateful, but after a while, they could see how they were being used. They started to speak up more. Brown did not like them coming in with their own lawyers, but he doesn't have much choice. Now the players have some defense against him.

I finally got myself some defense against Willie. Being left on my own made me think a lot. That's how I became religious. I was just wasting away. Life was nothing. I lived for Willie to come home off the road. To be a family again. One day you're a family at the park having a good time. The next day you're sitting by yourself at home. Just you and the children. Watching the TV screen, alone in bed.

I began to think, "What is life all about?" It was a big bore. A drag. I hated it. That lonesomeness was unbearable. When we first got married, I was just plain happy to be married. But after a while, I began to wish I was married to a garbage man who comes home every night.

My mother had studied as a Jehovah's Witness when I was a girl. She used to try to make me believe too, but I could only pretend. When my mother lost interest, I was glad. Now this religion is the center of my life. Our job is to preach the good news. In order to have the good news, the bad has to come first. There is destruction and a new coming. I am going to be saved, because I was baptized two years ago at Yankee Stadium. I climbed up a ladder into a five-foot-tall tub and got in. Immersion. That's how I found myself.

I go to five meetings a week. Most of them are for study, lectures, and talks. Our meetings are to get an accurate knowledge of the one time God and to spread the Word. On Thursdays, I go from door to door in the ministry. When I say my name, people ask if I am related to Willie. They say, "Are you *the* Mrs. Stargell?" Then they think: Gee, I'll listen for a while. Because of Willie. They don't care about the Bible one way or the other. They want to talk about baseball. If they are not interested in what we have to offer, I cut it short and go on to the next door.

"Now that I'm studying again, my mother says, "Why'd you pick that?" She thinks I'm too good to go around telling people about God. She says, "Did you go knocking on someone's door today? It's too cold out there for you. You're too good for that."

Dock Ellis's wife Paula was a good friend of mine. We used to discuss religion. She used to say, "I don't care about your Jehovah's Witnesses." When she split up with Dock, she moved to California and really got into religion. Now she is happy. I recommend the faith to other players' wives. Of course, this is my firm belief for anyone, but us wives particularly need something to help us get through the hell of baseball. Our men are gone six months of the year. I don't know about the other wives, but winter is just as bad as summer for me.

I hate having Willie home every day in the winter. When he is in the house, he finds things to complain about. Like keeping the house nice. I say he likes to keep the house immaculate. He says he doesn't. Just clean—"All you have to do is make up the beds and wash the dishes." Willie thinks I'm lazy, but I tell him I do what I can and if that's not good enough for him, too bad. We get in little arguments and I'll get mad and he'll start teasing. We've never not spoke for any length of time, because I can't stay mad and he can't either. We usually laugh at the end.

During the off season, Willie gets all tied up with football. He has his friends over and they watch games. They used to start hollering, "How's the chance of getting a little snack?" Ten or fifteen guys. That's like cooking two meals and I just didn't feel like it. I thought it was unfair. These guys all have TVs in their own homes. So they started a rotation, which was good, because it got them out of my house.

I used to feel like shooting the set when Willie turned on that damn football, but last winter, I tried to understand the game. I didn't get too far, but at least I could sit with him. When Willie watches football, he is at home.

Willie got involved with sickle cell anemia and that kept him out of the house all day long. When Willie gets caught up in something, he goes gung-ho. I hate anything that takes all his time. I felt for the people with sickle cell, but I got to the point where I didn't give a damn if everybody dropped dead of the disease. If everybody died, Willie would be home with me all the time. It's a selfish way of thinking, but if you wanted your man to be home with you, how else would you think about it? Either Willie likes all this activity or he's a glutton for punishment.

I don't really know Willie that well. I used to try and figure him out, but Willie is a very secretive person. Very private. He keeps things from me. I don't think he is hiding anything or covering up. It's just his personality. In this day and age it's odd that Willie is as private as he is. Everyone else spills all the beans all the time.

Willie wonders what we are going to do ten years from now. He would like to be part of baseball if there's a spot open for him when he is ready to retire. I would like to see him stay in the game, because that's his life. That's all Willie knows. He's been playing ball since he was ten.

If Willie went from an active player to an inactive player, there would be a tremendous drop in income. Coaches don't make nearly as much as ballplayers do. I think they make around twenty thousand. We could never live off that amount. We would be poverty-stricken. I don't think too much about the future, because I know the world is going to end.

It all seems so fruitless at times. Here we are moving to a new house and buying new furniture. Next year we plan to put in a pool. Lord only knows how long it will be there if our predictions are true and the end comes in 1975. This is 1973 already. I get confused sometimes and say, "What the heck." I still have to live, so I continue what we're doing and try not to think. If I did, I would come to a screeching halt and stop everything and go out and preach twenty-four hours a day.

I talk to Willie about God. He takes me seriously. He even told me he'd go door to door. One of these days, he is going to convert, because he is a good person. Then Willie and I will come together.

**Willie and Dee are talking together on one
of Willie's off days in Pittsburgh. They sit
at a bar in a downstairs den and sip wine.**

Willie: Do you have to go out tonight?

Dee: Yes, at seven-thirty. We have a meeting. [*kidding*] You know it keeps me out of trouble. I did doorbells yesterday.

Willie: I'll give you an hour a day for yourself!

Dee: I love going to ministry school. We playact our house calls. I'll get someone to be my partner and pretend we're going to a house to convert someone. I step out on a platform and take a subject, like getting discouraged knocking on doors. My partner says, "What's the matter, Dee?" I'll say, "I'm so discouraged. I think I'll just quit the ministry school. I'll just quit trying to warn people."

    Then she'll try to imitate the things that Jesus Christ did. We'll read the scripture to the congregation. And then I'll say, "I feel much better now and I think I'll continue with my work."

Willie: I worried about having people slam the door and spit in your face.

Dee: That makes me feel good! It makes me feel like I'm doing the right thing.

Willie: But there are so many nuts that see a young, lovely lady coming up to their door and who knows . . . that could be somebody just waiting to see a female. You expect people to react in good taste, but . . .

Dee: The preacher comes with us.

Willie: But what if they say . . .

Dee: We usually go into territories they've been in before. Someone will say, "Watch out for this one." They know the quacks. Or, "Don't be surprised if this man curses you out." Almost everywhere, you're sheltered. Almost every door we go to, we know what kind of person is behind it. What kind of reaction to expect. Like I know one man that's really crazy. I stay away.

Willie: What happens if some freak invites you in because you're a single lady.

Dee: If they invite you in, they know you're there for a purpose. If it's a man there, then we have a brother go with us.

It's really fun, Willie. I'm going to get you to do it one day. Sometimes you knock on the door and they say, "Who is it?" "Jehovah's Witnesses from the Watchtower Bible Society." They say, "Good-bye." In other words, they don't want to be bothered so you just go on.

I've come to doors where they say, "Is that right?" They're so happy to see you. You try and start a Bible study with them so they can gain an adequate knowledge of the Bible. Usually we'll start with a scripture like Second Peter II: 9. They say, "Seems that God is slow in cleaning up the earth. How come he hasn't put a stop to crooked politics?" Then you'll explain that he's taking his time, because he's giving a chance for everyone to see the truth. Just like Jonah and the whale. God used him to go to the city of Nineveh to tell all the people that they better change their ways or their city would be destroyed and all the people in it. Jonah didn't want to go with the Word. He pretended he was starting off and then he said, "No. I don't want to do that." That's when Jehovah caused the boat to rock. The men on the boat threw him into the sea and he was swallowed by a big fish called a whale. After he repented and said he was sorry, Jonah said, "I'll go tell the people now."

He warned the people of Nineveh that their city was going to be destroyed. All the people in the city repented. Even the king. Kings back in those days were pretty wicked. God didn't kill all the people, because he was showing mercy. The moral of the story is that people can change their ways and be forgiven. There's hope for you yet, Wilver Stargell!

Willie: I doubt it.

Dee: Do you have hope to go to heaven when you die? What do you think happens to the dead?

Willie: I'm just worried about winning tomorrow.

Dee: But there won't be no tomorrow if you don't repent. I'm kidding. But this is such a good way to keep yourself strong. You have the Bible behind you. We keep upbuilding each other.

Willie: Sometimes I think that those religious people are just after money.

Dee: But no one in our congregation says, "Don't forget the contribution." If you give a hundred dollars a week, your name goes on top of the list. But you can give fifty cents.

Willie: Church I went to out in California, they locked the door until they'd gotten as much money as they wanted. Had guys standing by the doors. They sold stale loaves of bread for a hundred dollars. Minister pulls up in a Rolls-Royce and they roll out the carpet.

Dee: Just like Billy Graham. He speaks real good, but he's not telling the whole truth. He's always shouting dollars and having people spend all their money. All that money goes to him and I don't think that's right.

　　　With our group, they never force you to pay. It's so simple and basic. There's no big words. We are simply supposed to do the will of God.

Willie: How 'bout the will of Will?

Dee: You should take this more seriously. I'm trying to teach our children. I'm amazed that they go to the meetings and sit still. They don't know what it's all about, but they know when they go to Kingdom Hall, they're supposed to be quiet. They're terrible all week.

Willie: I don't give you much help, honey.

Dee: I always wanted my kids to be like other kids—so well-brought-up and well-mannered. But then I realized I had to get myself together first and then take care of the kids. I wish you were around more, Willie.

Willie: Got to pay the bills now, honey. But I won't play ball forever.

Dee: Then I'm going to get you. You'll convert!

**Dee goes upstairs to finish cooking dinner and Willie reflects on their relationship.**

Willie: Dee and I have a good sex life. That's one thing we've never had any problem about. I've played my share in fooling around with girls. It used to be just a sex thing. I had nothing in common with them. Just girls here and girls there. But then I got a sense of guilt that I was using people. I found myself telling little lies to sound impressive. I'd say, "I'll be calling you." That kind of jazz. I was getting bored and began to look into a person's mind to see what we had in common. If you can be with a girl and talk, then you're coming together on a mentality level. If there's a sexual, physical attraction, then it will be that much better. Now I find that I want to be with a girlfriend even if she's menstruating. So many men are turned off and look for someone else. I want to be with a person, and any time the two of us are together it's pleasant. That's what I look for.

It takes a unique woman to be married to a ballplayer. Dee sits in that house and pulls her hair out. I'm out traveling around the world, eating in restaurants with the temptation of other women. These thoughts must go through her mind, with the kids, the phone ringing, and dogs barking. When she finally gets the kids to bed, she has to wash the dishes and I happen to call while she's out. "Where in the hell have you been all day?" *I* ask.

Dee has been looking for something to believe in. Religion is a way of mind. She wants to know more about Christ. She didn't feel she was getting it from the Baptist or Methodist churches, so she took on this challenge as a Jehovah's Witness. I wouldn't say Dee was lonely and found religion. Dee does have an abundance of time, but she could have taken up knitting, bowling, or tennis. I'm only out of town six months of the year. A traveling salesman is gone for twelve. You should learn to live with separation.

Dee should *not* have to learn to be shoved around. I don't like getting direct attention when we're out together. People knock Dee over to get to me. I got to pick Dee up out of the mud and say, "Honey, you understand," but I don't.

*I* have no complaints about being married. I need the support of my family. I don't think I give them enough. I don't want Dee as a housekeeper, a babysitter, and a cook. Before we got married, Dee said she'd like to be my friend, my buddy, my wife, my girlfriend, my shoulder, my school chum, and one of the guys. That's what I was looking for. Of course, I was a fantasy for Dee, but we got down to ground pretty fast. I learned that love is a communication and understanding and trust. When there's a problem, and one mind's going in one direction while the other's flying away, you've got to find a happy medium. Dee and I are working toward a better understanding.

Since I've been involved in sickle cell, I haven't even been at home during the winter. Dee realizes that there's a need for me to help, but I do neglect home. I'd like to be a father and a husband. Not ninety-eight-percent humanitarian and two-percent family man. I'm always out there helping. Dee says when someone wants to go to the bathroom, they call me. I'm a grinder in the winter, making public appearances and clinics, but we could all be doing these things together. I say, "I'll let you sit here until I get back." In two or three days I'll get back and someone else calls and I go away again. I never spend time at home. I don't even do the odds and ends around the house. Dee and I talk a lot. I'm concerned about my home life, even though I have an itch to travel and move, to meet different people.

I love to have fun and be playful. I take pride in what I do. I feel that everything should have a delicate touch to it, including home runs. A quick snap at the wrist. That's where you get your distance from. You can almost hear the bat whistle. It's not done with any strain. I'd like to have that caring and grace in my life at home. I don't right now, but I'm going to try.

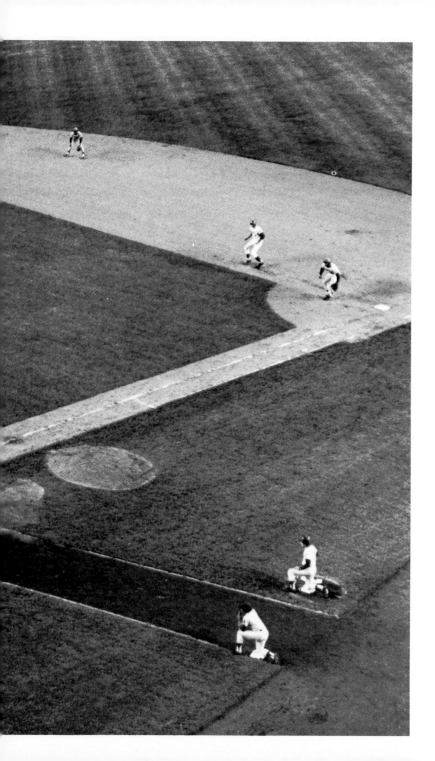

# The Season

**The Pirates' general manager Joe Brown is considered one of the fairest managers in major-league baseball. The players said that he never traded out of spite. This year, Brown's failure to trade at all has been questioned, particularly since the club has had such an erratic pitching record.**

**Brown attended almost all the ball games and traveled with the team on the road. He relaxes in a restaurant one evening before leaving for Shea Stadium.**

Brown: I have always felt like a father to the players. When I started in baseball, I wasn't actually old enough to be a father, but I worked and strained and sweated about every one of my boys.

My own father was an athlete. When he was nine, he was an aerial trapeze artist. He played baseball in 1941 in northeast Ohio, where he was a pretty good fielder and could run. He certainly was a fierce competitor. My mother said he would come home smashed up with a black eye. Got in a fight in a ball game.

Athletics is all I have ever known. When I was ten and we moved from the East to the West, I used to work out with a San Francisco Double A team. I saw all the DiMaggios and Ted Williams. I took a road trip with them every year. There are a lot of wonderful people in baseball!

I left UCLA in my sophomore year and went to work for the White Sox. I spent fifteen years in the minor leagues before I came to Pittsburgh. I do have an understanding of what the player has to go through. They complain to me, "Gee, I spent four years in the minors." After my *thirteenth* year in the minors, I was making four hundred and twenty-five dollars a month. But time is not against a man in the front office. It is against the players. Their life is short. That is a big difference.

The minors will never be replaced by college baseball, because there is no pressure on a college baseball player. No crowds of any size. The football player has self-inflicted pressure because of the draft choice. Our own organization drafts many more high-school players than college players. We have never gotten much from the draft, because when you finish at the top, you get last choice. The Holtzmans go pretty early.

Baseball players start young. If they haven't made it by the time they're twenty-two, they probably won't. Take our club. Milt May was in the major leagues at twenty. Bob Robertson at twenty-one. Bob Moose at nineteen. Rennie Stennett at twenty. Cash at twenty-one. Hebner, twenty-one; Willie, twenty-two; Oliver, twenty-one.

Most athletes are at their best between twenty-seven and thirty-one.

They have always had the physical skills and as they get older, they can control them. Jim Rooker is peaking at thirty-one, but he used to have a reputation as a drinker. He has gotten himself under control. We didn't even have to speak to him.

Willie resented it when we said he had to lose weight three years ago, but his success in the past few years has come from keeping his weight down. You have to keep your body in shape, because your body is your living. Willie made real sacrifices, but look at his performance. He's in better shape now than he has been in five years. His weight is down and his body is hard. Baseball is a physical game. You have to care about yourself on and off the field. If you let yourself go, somewhere along the line your body doesn't back you up. You can't even begin the task of performing.

However, being successful or not in the major leagues is primarily based on your psychological, mental approach to the game. The difference in talent between San Diego and Pittsburgh, Philadelphia and Cincinnati isn't all that great. Winning depends on belief in yourself, coordinated effort and a desire to succeed. When I scout, you give me the guy who really wants to fight, and, if he has any kind of ability, I will take him and he'll make it.

Thirty years ago, the players spent more time thinking about playing than they do now. Players are still tremendously dedicated, especially the Latin and black players. They need the game. Although society is getting closer to equality, we are still a long way from it. The opportunity to be successful in the entertainment community is much greater than it is in the business world. Baseball is entertainment.

I have always felt that the best player ought to be in every position whether he is black, green or yellow. People give me that horse manure about fielding a black team every day. I think back to Los Angeles who played five or six blacks. And San Francisco—Pagan, McCovey, Mays. They have drawn the fans. I think people look for quality, not color now. Our game is based on winning. If you look at nothing but dollars, you only make dollars for success. Who is the most popular player in Pittsburgh today? Bob Robertson or Willie Stargell? One is an Anglo-Saxon with red hair. The other is black. But Willie is by far the most popular player we have on the ballclub. It is not just Willie's performance that sets him apart. People recognize the humanness of the fellow.

There are whites on our club who think the blacks are given preference. And there are blacks who think the whites are preferred. Every athlete has a built-in ego that is bigger than he is. There is no way he will admit that the other guy is better than him. So he looks for an excuse. "He plays, because I am black." I have been associated with athletes all my life and the need for self-confidence is tremendous.

I have had some terrible players on this club, who thought they were

better than Babe Ruth. They went back to the minor leagues and said they were getting screwed by Pittsburgh. We sent them to Triple A and they still couldn't make it. I wish some of the wonderful talent we've had could muster that supreme confidence. That makes a major-league player. With ability!

I remember Willie when he first came up. One day in spring training Willie was at batting practice and he put on a show. In thirty swings, he hit twelve or fifteen balls out of the park. When he got through, he had a standing ovation. As a result of batting practice! The fans knew they were looking at something special. There wasn't any doubt early in Willie's career that this was the finest talent to come to Pittsburgh in years. Murtaugh used to say, "He has a loud bat. I can tell when Stargell's hitting even if my back is turned."

Willie was hungry when he came up. I knew he had financial problems, but I don't think his desire was for money. Willie has always been a low-keyed person. He gives his all, but he's not loud. Willie doesn't try to impress anyone, but Willie is prideful. He carried the club in 1971 until the playoffs when he had trouble with his knees, but there was never an alibi. He was the best I ever saw him. He'd been a great player and it was the greatest self-control I've ever seen. He doesn't take advantage in his relations with other people. Even when he hits forty home runs. He's a special guy with special kinds of antennae. He's sensitive.

Willie leads by performance. He also plays when other people wouldn't. Not only when he's not feeling well, but when he's hurting. He's the outstanding player on our ballclub. He has the sanity on the club. He makes it easier for other fellows to have the proper perspective. Some players have Willie's attitude, too. Like Dave Cash. I'm sure he's unhappy that he's not playing regularly, but he knows if he sounds off publicly or in the clubhouse, it could hurt the ballclub. Dave is adult enough to talk to Virdon or me. We're the only people who can make the changes to satisfy him. Not everybody is that adult.

The difference between finishing first and second is ten thousand dollars, If we get out of the pennant race, all hell will break loose. Everyone will complain. Certain players don't realize that if they're fifth spear carrier for Pittsburgh, they'll also be the fifth spear carrier for San Diego.

I thought Alley was physically sound and had a good attitude this year, but he was plain scared. He thought he was going to get hurt. He was a real loss. Then too many people over-reacted to the death of Clemente and felt that they personally had to make up for his loss. They had to hit for a higher average and more home runs. They didn't analyze their abilities. Rennie and Manny got too power-conscious, and now they're both below average.

When Clemente was here, Oliver had a much easier job as a center-fielder. He just had to cover the left-field side. Most balls are in right center and Clemente would get them. Zisk has done a fine job, but he's a long way from being a Clemente. Who isn't? Zisk has developed as a better ballplayer. He is more accurate and he's always had good hands. I always felt that Zisk would be an adequate outfielder and I'm sure he'll hit thirty to forty home runs a year. Both Richies on our team have amazing power.

Baseball is the hardest game to play. The difference between hitting the ball and missing it is just a fraction of an inch. Making a tackle and a pass is not. There is no boxscore for a linebacker. No one measures the number of tackles he should have made and didn't. There are measures by which you tell the efficiency of a player in baseball. They aren't always true. A player who hits three hundred is not always better than a player who hits two seventy, but generally you can tell the value of a man by his statistics. You can't in football.

Baseball is a statistic game. A record game. Look what they've done with Hank Aaron. You can't compare apples with oranges, but there is a constancy to the record even if the circumstances are slightly different. That's one thing about our game. When Babe Ruth hit his sixty home runs, the pitcher was still sixty feet, six inches from the plate.

The guy who invented this game was lucky or a genius. He either took a slide rule or studied for a hundred years. In so many plays, the runner is thrown out by a fraction of an inch. How many guys are *just* safe at second? Happens all the time. You *just* miss a pitch over the mound. Why wasn't it fifty feet, six inches, or ninety feet from the plate to the mound? Why weren't the bases a hundred eighty feet apart? Those of us who are in a position to change the game haven't, because we realize it's a hell of a game as is. As you get older, you like to think young. There's been a lot of talk about getting more action, but that's apples and oranges. We're not football. We're not basketball. We're baseball and we're different. I don't know why we can't be. Why do we have to have a frenetic pace all the time? To people who don't know the game and can't appreciate the nuances, at times the game seems slow. Slowness and casualness are baseball. People go to football games who don't know what the hell is going on. And if they do, they can't use their knowledge until after the game is over, because everything is such a conglomeration on the field that you can't appreciate strategy. The pitcher—the batter. That's a great strategy. A great confrontation. Willie says when he faces Seaver it's like two rocks grinding against each other.

I have to make money, so my job is to win. If you win, you can make money. My job is not to change the game, but to change the attitude of the news media and the general public.

This is my thirty-fifth year in baseball and I've never gotten a letter about the length of the game. The people who harp on the length are the people who cover it. They want to get home at nine-thirty, not eleven. Young sportswriters write negatively. It's easy to be a negative writer. You could find faults with Jesus Christ. It takes a great writer to make something interesting out of something good. A sportswriter who's making eight or nine thousand dollars a year wants to find out something bad about Willie Stargell, who's making better than a hundred. Most of the young guys don't love the game. Today their work is a business. Football's at the top now. Baseball was number one for so many years.

If you watch baseball over a period of time, you come to know the character of the individual player. You can tell a hell of a lot about a person by the way he plays. There's an electric something that happens between the fans and the players. Even if I went to a strange ballpark, within a couple of innings, there'd be somebody who was *my* ballplayer. Jose Pagan. I thought he was the living end. You walk into a football game and all you see is fellows with hoods over their heads. You can't tell whether a player is black or white. In basketball, everyone's moving so fast that you don't have an opportunity to see the personality of the man.

Baseball players tend not to be educated, but I don't think that affects character. Twenty years ago, players were more dedicated, more driven toward success. Now instead of thinking about success, they think about the dollars first. "How much money can I get?" Not, "How much can I contribute?" If you contribute enough, you're going to get paid well.

Baseball is life in a fishbowl. Everything in our society floats in that bowl. It happens to be in public view. In baseball, you can see more clearly, because the shortness of a player's career exaggerates his life. Failure and success are magnified. The struggle to the top through hard work and application. Friendships. Compromise and conviction. What else is there? Baseball is life.

**As a major-leaguer for eleven years,
Willie is invited to talk to a group of
women who are starting a professional
baseball league. Willie discusses the
problems of managing a ballclub.**

Willie: You ladies plan to start at the very top with major league ball. The public
must want to see everything you're doing. If you are not at your best and
you're completely unorganized, then it will be just a matter of time before
they throw you out of the ballpark. But after you have observed a spring
training next year and asked the purpose for all the players' activities, then
you can formulate your plans.

Knowing something about baseball would help you a lot. It is hard to
imagine what a manager has to go through and what he looks for in his
ballclub. I can talk from the player's standpoint, but you are going to have to
go through coaches, managers, general managers, assistant general managers, scouts, and treasurers. The Commissioner can tell you only so much
about how you are supposed to run a complete league. The Commission is
owned by the owners and the Players Association represents the players.
We are always in conflict with the owners, so you will have a division there.

If you got three hundred and fifty people coming to spring training, how
many are you going to send contracts to? Since they're just starting out, are
you going to invite women to spring training and then see who you sign to
contract? Are you going to have contracts on a yearly basis or a tentative
contract where, if you do what we expect in thirty days, then we'll give you a

bonus; if you don't, we'll let you go? If you have tentative contracts, the player has a goal to shoot for and you have a chance to look at her. If she is as good as you think she is, you don't mind giving a bonus, but if she's not, you don't have to put up with her all year.

You have suggested having a team psychiatrist, but if you have coaches for instructors, you won't have time to deal with the players' emotional problems. The players will have to keep their personal problems at home. Presumably, they will be professional people.

You are going to find that you have players that are not good for the club, but they're producing. That's a big decision to make—what to do with that person. As managers, your job is to keep people coming to the stadium. Your main concern is the turnstile. You can't pamper one player and keep the fans away from the ballpark because she's making a mess for the team.

Then you will find that players need money, advances, and financial assistance. You've got to be geared for that. If you have a player that says she needs ten thousand dollars to get herself straight and it would help her from a mental standpoint, would you loan her money? When you start in this business, you must anticipate that problem.

As you look for a manager, you have to watch for several qualities. Regardless of what sex they are, you have to find somebody that can command respect rather than demand it, and that knows how to treat people as people. She has got to get the best out of the players. If you are going to have a twenty-five-player roster, then she must keep them that's not playing happy, and when they do get an opportunity to play, to be willing to play. When you talk about a manager, you're talking about a mother, father, friend, and enemy. Plus a lady that's not going to go crazy in the middle of the baseball season.

You only need four coaches. Two will be on the lines. The coach in the bullpen makes sure that the pitchers are warming up properly and she should detect anybody that's having problems and suggest whether they should be pitching or not. If the manager calls down and needs a pitcher, she will say to warm up the left-hander and the right-hander. If the bullpen coach sees the right-hander isn't throwing well, she can call back, "I don't advise this guy to be throwing because she doesn't seem to be throwing as good as I thought she would." If you are under the impression that she can perform and her stuff is nappy, your whole game can blow open.

Then you have one more coach that sits with the manager. That's usually the pitching coach. She watches the pitching and goes out to the mound when she is needed. She also gives the signs. The other team expects the manager to give signs, so the manager likes to tell the coach. Or the manager might give them herself and let the coach pretend. This creates mass confusion if the other team is trying to read the signs.

You have to have hard lieutenants that constantly keep the girls grinding, but you should get people who try to have some fun at ball. Although it's hard work, I know *I'm* doing what I really enjoy!

**After the meeting, Willie reflects on women's baseball.**

Willie: I find it difficult to talk to these girls. For some reason, they think I'm trying to say, "You can't do it." Still they come to me: "Well, we're determined, no matter what you say." I am not being facetious. I'm coming off the shoulder with everything I tell them. I even have to watch how I phrase "the players" instead of "the girls," although I do slip up. "Miss Attitude," she got up: "Excuse me." She didn't even want to sit next to me, a man. These women haven't the slightest idea of what they are headed for.

I was telling them, "When you get a team, you've got to make travel arrangements and have a charter plane." They said, "Oh, we never thought of that." You can't make a major-league team travel on a bus from here to San Francisco or Los Angeles!

Their financial backing is a secret they're trying to keep from me. I'm not asking, "Where are you getting the money from?" I'm just saying, "You're going to have to figure on a payroll, administration costs, travel arrangements, uniforms, and equipment. You can't expect a dozen balls to go for a whole year. Or a dozen bats." Every player will want their own personalized bat. Once a woman finds out that she is a major-leaguer, she'll be smart. She will compare what other major-leaguers are doing and how they are being treated. These women are going to want the same treatment. They are even going to want salaries! You could operate a semipro baseball team on a whole different basis, but on a professional level, they will expect nothing less than professional treatment. They will have to stay in the best hotels.

I didn't want to be the one to say, "Hey, you just can't do it. Don't even think about it." But I wonder about the problems. Parents start throwing a baseball to their sons as soon as they can walk. They bring them up, brainwash them, and put them in various baseball leagues. Every parent knows that he has a professional baseball player coming in the family. It is crazy for women to think they can start without all this background. Girls are just beginning to play Little League ball.

A guy who has a big chest has trouble getting around on an inside pitch. That hand has to come all the way through. If you have anything tying you up, you're going to be an off-paced hitter. Think of certain types of women. If they keep *them* off the team, they'll be accused of discrimination!

I do not see how women can pitch. Most pitchers have pitched all their lives and they still get a sore arm. These women don't even know the significance of a sore arm. If you pitch with one, it can damage certain muscles permanently.

The girls are banking on playing in Three Rivers Stadium. They say, "We can schedule it so when you all are on the road, we can play." I said, "If you think for one minute that Mr. Joe Brown is going to say, 'I'm going to let you play here,' you're crazy." If the Pirates aren't playing good ball and you people are outstanding and the attendance is going to you instead of the Pirates, he wouldn't even consider that." If I were Joe Brown, I'd say no.

Once they start inviting these different women to play, my wife would say, "I want to try out. I want to go to spring training for three months. You did it. What makes you think I can't?" Then what the hell is going to happen to the rest of the family? I am working too. I'm the man of the house. I'm supposed to work. I can see me getting up in the morning and fixing breakfast so Dee can go to the ballpark. And she leaves passes for *me* to sit with the kids. She have a bad night and I have to put up with *her*!

I am trying to help these women. Not to discourage them, but to be very honest. I say, "I told you everything. Now it's up to you to decide."

**Willie recaps the last week against
Philadelphia and talks about the team.**

Willie: In Philadelphia on Monday [May 21], Carlton made some real good pitches, but he wasn't throwing the balls good as last year! He threw me some sliders. Then they got a four-run lead. We came back and tied the score. In the top of the ninth, we were one ahead, and got them out in the bottom. It was real good for Steve Blass to get the win. He's had such a hard time this year. We all have. But in the last couple of days, we came back with some big wins. That game in New York where we won in the tenth was a real big one for us.

I hit a fast ball, up a little bit, for my twelfth homer this year. I was just looking for something hard and fortunate enough to get all my stuff going at the right time. With the impact of the bat speed and the ball speed, the ball carried for a great distance. But I would rather home runs not necessarily go so far. When they do, the pitchers bear down that much more. They say, "You'll never get that pitch again." And that particular pitch is etched on their brain forever.

Besides the homer, I hit into an outstanding double play, I flew out to center and I grounded out hard to second base. I am making contact with the ball, so I feel that groove coming on again. I lost it for awhile.

I always believe in getting my cuts in. Can't hit the ball if you don't swing, and I like to hit. If a batter hits three out of ten times up, then he bats three hundred. If Joe Namath completed three out of every ten passes, he'd be canned. The odds are against you in baseball, but you learn to live with averages. Still I figure every time I get up to the plate I'm going to get a hit. I give my best. I don't like to make an out, but when it happens, I do not let the anger and frustration last for more than a minute. It does not affect me the next time I'm up. I can't help feeling that if I go four for four, I will go five for five. I am an optimist.

If a pitcher I know is on the mound, I don't take the first pitch, because I have hit against him from time to time and have an idea of the velocity of his pitches. Since I hit fourth, I can watch him pitch against three other guys.

On Tuesday [May 22] Dock was throwing real good, even though this was his fifth straight loss. When Philadelphia got hits off him, the balls weren't hit that well. They were just good enough to go through the middle and cause the damage they did. A ball hit to me went into the lights. I couldn't see it. When it came down, it hit my glove and landed on the ground, so they charged me with an error. I'm just glad the ball didn't hit me in the head.

Twitchell threw a beautiful game. His pitches were extremely hard and to spots. We talked about how he was pitching and just waited for a mistake. Twitchell didn't make any. Pitchers have their good days too!

We need to play a month without any rain. Rain affects the ball club, because the guys don't get a chance to hit and the pitchers don't throw. We got rained out Sunday and Wednesday this week. When we are playing every day, we maintain a rhythm. Then we can get back in the groove. If we don't play every day, nothing jells. That's why we're losing. The sun would help us to win.

Robertson has been having knee problems, so Virdon took him out. He has had bad knees all along. When you play on turf, you're going to have bad knees whether you have them or not. A day's rest may do Robertson some good. Some clubs can't afford to rest a starter, but we have a deep club with backup men, so we can.

Robertson will have a complicated summer because of his condition. I know what he is going through, because I had a problem with my left knee in 1971. I know his injury is serious. He could either go and have an operation or deal with the pain. Like most stubborn athletes, he will deal with the pain. It's just one miserable feeling. Being hurt takes all the fun out of the game, because even though you try not to think about the pain while you're out playing, you cannot concentrate on what you do.

The team is crazy as hell. Even though we have been losing and had low moments, there never has been a sign of panic in the clubhouse. After playing together for so many years, we know we are capable of playing better ball. We just haven't been hitting, we haven't been playing very good defense, and we haven't had good pitching. We are doing all the things we shouldn't be doing.

I didn't play this Sunday against the Astros, because they wanted to rest the old man. This season, I won't play the night game after the day game or vice versa. But we finally had a beautiful day. Thought the rain was going to be a factor, because it started cloudy and sprinkling. We thought we'd be lucky if we got five innings in. All of a sudden the sun burst through, got as high as seventy-five. If the weather holds this week for our home stand, we go to Houston for three days. It's sure there will be no rain in the Astrodome!

**May 28.**
Pittsburgh beats Houston in Pittsburgh. Dock Ellis halts his streak of pitching losses at five as the Pirates post a 4–2 victory.

**May 29.**
Stargell hits his thirteenth homer of the season. Pirates over Atlanta, 6–1.

**May 30.**
Pittsburgh 4–Atlanta 2.
The Pirates' third straight victory. They move into second place in the Eastern Division.

**May 31.**
With his fourteenth home run, Stargell leads the majors. The ball landed in the upper deck of Three Rivers Stadium, an area reached only three times before, each time by Stargell. Atlanta goes down to Pittsburgh, 3 to 1.

**May Monthly record: 13–14.**

**June 1.**
Stargell hits number fifteen. Pittsburgh's fifth straight triumph is a 9–6 victory over Cincinnati. One paper says, "That distinct rumble you hear in the NL East is probably the Pirates, waking up at last."

**June 2.**
The Pirates make it six straight wins, defeating Cincinnati 4–3.

**June 3.**
The Pirates are set back, as Cincinnati wins.

**June 4.**
Stargell raps his sixteenth homer, but the Pirates lose again, downed by San Francisco 7–2.

**June 5.**
San Francisco 3–Pittsburgh 2.

**June 6.**
Steve Blass lasts only two innings, as Pittsburgh is again defeated by San Francisco, 9–7. Virdon says, "Blass may have to go to the bullpen for a while."

**June 7.**
Off day.

**June 8.**
At Houston, Pittsburgh loses 4–3. Stargell hits number seventeen.

**June 9.**
The Pirates end a five-game skid, beating Houston.

**June 10.**
The Pirates' June swoon resumed, Houston 7–Pittsburgh 1.

**June 11 through June 13.**
The Pirates lose three games to Atlanta and are pummeled 18–3 on the last night. They drop into fifth place in the NL East and have lost nine out of the last ten games.

**June 14.**
Off day.

**June 15.**
Cincinnati defeats the Pirates in a rain-stalled game. Sanguillan returns to catching and Clines goes from the bench to right field.

*Johnny Bench and friends*

# At Cincinnati on Old Timer's Day

*Casey Stengel and Bill Virdon*

**Third baseman Richie Hebner is on the field early before the afternoon game.**

Richie: I ran into Pete Rose's boy in the dugout. I teased him: "We're going to beat your father's team today. You tell your old man that we're gonna whip him!" When I asked the kid who he's rooting for today, he said, "My dad." I ask, "Who else?" Kid says, "Nobody." I always talk to kids because they're fun.

This glove I have is falling apart. I got it in 1967. No one ever said a thing about it until a month ago when I was signing autographs in New York. These Little Leaguers with brand-new gloves leaned over the railing and said, "Do you play with that thing?" I have made errors with my glove and I'll make a lot more, but it's a good glove and I like it. Don't know how long it will last. Some wise guy wrote, "Please retire me," on the heel.

To play professional ball, you have to have a little temper in you. I may have too much, but I'm getting better. The sportswriters just get on me. I am easy to pick on. I'm the only one on the team that's not married. I get paid good money and drive a new car. People get jealous, I guess.

I am jealous of guys that play hockey, because I think that's the greatest sport going. I work out with the Pittsburgh Penguins in the winter. Hockey is my kind of sport. You can get your feelings out on the ice. Baseball is you and the pitcher. Strike out and you gotta go back to the dugout and wait until your next time up. That's why I throw my helmet around sometimes. I can't stand all those feelings inside me. That's the trouble with ball. There's no outlet in the game.

88

I do like some things about baseball. Stan Musial came out with a beautiful statement at the old-timers' game today. He says, "Geez, they still got all these lefties out here. Those pitchers went through World War Two. They have got to be sharp."

I would like to win today. If we could at least split tomorrow and take four games with the Cubs and four games with the Mets, we would be way out of the bottom next week. I am not used to losing. It's bad for my temper.

Clines: Now I don't have to worry about pinch-hitting. That's the worst feeling in the world. You sit on the bench for seven or eight innings, then grab a bat and get up there and swing. I have never liked it. I'm not that type of player. Maybe if I were thirty-five or thirty-six years old I would be.

The Pirates don't know what I can do, because I have never been out on that field more than two weeks at a time. I only asked to be given an opportunity. If I go out and don't do a job, I won't say anything else.

Last year, I led the team in hitting. I batted three thirty-four, so I was very disappointed in spring training when I didn't get a plain chance for the job in right field. They said they wanted to experiment. They really wanted to get Milt May in the lineup. In this game, your career is so short that I was mad I wasn't getting a clean shot at the job.

I played one game in right field in the spring. They played me in center, but they knew Oliver would be there. I wasn't asking for a job. I was asking for a chance. They denied me until a couple of days ago when Virdon said I was going to right. Of course, I had been blasting to the press. Why should I sit around and wait because Joe Brown's too stubborn to trade me? You can't have your cake and eat it too. That's the lesson I was trying to get Joe Brown to understand. I want to play and I can play every day. Brown was holding me back.

During the early winter, Brown tried to trade me. Then Roberto died. If they had traded me, there wouldn't be somebody who could play all the outfield positions. I can hit and run and throw. Brown's probably proud that he was shrewd enough not to let me go.

Why I wasn't given a chance for right field is a question that has never been answered. Virdon told me they wanted more power in the lineup, which isn't true. You have to have a chance to hit the ball before you can tell whether you are or aren't a power hitter. And Milt May is no power-hitter anyway. He didn't hit one home run last year.

Manny Sanguillan is the best catcher in baseball. I think so. Management thinks so. Why move the best to another position when I could have played right field? My personal opinion is that they wanted some blond hair and blue eyes on the diamond. We have only started nine black players one time in Pittsburgh and that caused some controversy. The fans wrote in and the press made a big play: "It's the first time in history they ever started nine black ballplayers." I didn't notice. Why should they? The game was against the Philadelphia Phillies in 1971 and, as a matter of fact, we won.

Every team has a spark plug that's going to keep players on their toes.

This is the type of game I play. I am daring. I'll do things other ballplayers won't try. Say there's a base hit up the middle and I'm on first. I'll go to second real hard. If I see the guy is slow on the ball, I'll take off for third and slide in. Then you have runners on first and third. When the other players see me do that, it puts a spark under them. Gets us all going. I have always done that for the club.

Last week when I talked to Virdon, he said that the players offered in trade for me would be an insult to him and me. That's wrong. I wouldn't care if they traded me for a dozen broken bats. I just wanted a chance to play. To get runs in. But they wouldn't think about Gene Clines. They only thought about what they could get from Gene Clines. I'm sure they could have found another pinch-hitter! Well, now's my chance to show them.

**Pitcher Dock Ellis lounges in the dugout before the double-header on Sunday afternoon.**

Dock: Willie Stargell is holding the team together this year, even though we're falling apart.

I've known Willie for eight years. First met him in '64. They called me up to Pittsburgh to play an exhibition game and Willie was driving down the street. I waved him down in the car and said, "You know me." He just said, "Let's go."

I said, "Where are we going?" He went to the grocery store and got some big steaks, about two and a half inches thick, and a nice bottle of wine. Then I should have caught on to how ballplayers keep their weight down, but at that time I was so skinny I didn't have to worry. I was about six foot three and a half and weighed a hundred seventy-two. Now I weigh one ninety-three, but I've been weighing two twenty. Gotta keep eating those big-league steaks. I had never seen steaks that big.

Willie wasn't married then, but he had a hell of a good cook. He tried to tell me to apply myself, but it was too soon for me to hear it. I used to be out on the streets every night. I never went to sleep before three in the morning. I was running myself down, but I didn't realize it. I was so young.

Now I don't have to go out at night. I just get on the phone. In different

cities, the chickaderos come right to me. Before I had to pound the pavements, looking for them.

I room by myself. Management tried to put a few guys with me, but I got 'em out. You used to have to room with someone, even if you paid for the room yourself. Putting me with older guys was a way to slow me down, but it didn't work. I can't stand to be in a room with any of them players. They're like women. Yak, yak, yak. I like to relax. Now I go to bed earlier and eat better food than I used to.

This afternoon, I've got me a chickadero in the stands, but I am supposed to keep the pitching record. Going to get myself kicked out of the game by vamping the umpire. Then I'll go to the stands.

**As the game starts, Dock leans out toward
the field and ribs the home-plate umpire.**

Dock: I'm the ballplayer's ballplayer. Just tell them to hurry up this game. That ball ain't low. Ball ain't high either. Both of you are midgets. That's what I wanna hear: strike! Make him get in the batter's box. He ain't supposed to have no time out. Strike! It ain't high. No way in the world that ball is high. It'll be off the plate. Good. Got an inferiority complex anyway, the little rascal. C'mon, Will. C'mon, Will. Hi, Richie!

He *did* swing, he *did* swing. You lookin' right at the damn thing, you can't even see the man swing at the ball. What kind of mess is that? Man swing at the ball. Standing right out there. Get out of that hole. Mickey Rooney. Popeye. You can't tell me what I see. I didn't tell you nothin'. I can tell you didn't see the ball. You didn't see him swing?

You gonna tell me to shut up? You ain't no school teacher. You the principal for the day? You supposed to umpire the game. Don't be listening to me. You listen to me, you'll go crazy. I can talk if I want to. I come into the world talking. Nobody had to spank me on the butt. Tell me to shut up. You can't kick me outta the game. Ain't no way in the world you gonna kick me outta the game. It's gonna look pretty funny to the president of the league, you kicking somebody out of the game 'cause they talking. Shut up you, and do your job. Jeez Christ. Feeney going to fire you. You outta your mind.

**The umpire calls Virdon on to the field and
Dock, to his personal satisfaction, is
removed from the game.**

**In the locker room after the Pirates have
lost three out of four games. They are
now in last place.**

An infielder: I feel like the afterbirth of a Mongolian jerk fuck. That's what I feel like. I feel like I was reincarnated. Besides, I'm a mother-fucking prick. A fuck-up.

Mama said there'd be days like this, but she didn't say there'd be that fucking many. Happy Father's Day. Horseshit day. I don't want to think any more. I quit thinking.

Another infielder: You just react. You just fucking react. You go by your emotions.

Infielder: I think we should go back to spring training.

Outfielder: We ain't played sixty games yet.

Another infielder: Can you get about four band-aids? I got cuts all over myself. There's just a little dirt out there, but the little dirt out there's like a fucking main street in your home town.

Outfielder: I came up in '63, so I know what it's like when the dudes are young. Ain't one thing to do but keep driving.

Another infielder: Keep driving?

Outfielder: You got bills to pay.

Reporter: You're the kind of suckers I've lost all my money on.

Another infielder: Should be smart enough not to bet your money. Put it in the bank. Buy the kids some shoes.

Reporter: What's wrong with you Pirates, you mother-fuckers? What do you think is wrong?

Willie: Not winning.

Reporter: Why aren't you winning?

Willie: We just in one of them things, that's all. You asking questions we ain't got no answers for.

Reporter: You think it can be turned around?

Willie: There's no question about it. We haven't played sixty games, you know. As long as we don't give up on ourselves, then we can definitely make a better showing. Hell, I've played when we're winning. I also know what you have to do in a situation like this. You just have to go out, play hard, and try not to worry about what happened yesterday.

Reporter: You think there's a danger if the team keeps losing . . .

Willie: You keep losing, you're in danger. But I don't think there's any certain time in terms of when we gotta start winning. I don't think we can go much longer on this basis. But we've got a home stand coming up . . .

Steve Blass: We just knocked the hell out of everybody for three years and enjoyed it. We are going through a rough period now. Gotta take it until we get things turned around. There is such a thin line between having success and not having success. You are not aware how thin the line is until you fall to the other side. When you start to struggle and drop your guard a little, that line jumps right up at you.

We can't let losing get easy to take. We have to keep fighting, keep going on forever and ever. I have all the confidence in the world, because I have done it. My arm feels well, so I know it will turn around. It is just a matter of how quickly I can get it going.

I feel disappointed, because I know I have a responsible position on the club and I want to do well. One of the reasons the team has been struggling is that I haven't been doing a damn thing.

Some days I feel good or go right. But not very often. Just enough to give me courage. My arm feels weak. I am preoccupied with selection of pitch and trying to throw the ball. I've had slumps before. I was two and eight at the beginning of one season. Then I finished ten and twelve. But I have never had a systematic slump like this. I haven't had a good game in the first twelve times I have started.

It makes me start wondering whether I'm doing sixteen different things mechanically wrong or whether I'm just starting to weigh down my mind. I've been reading some books on positive thinking to try to help myself.

My problem is control. I hurry too much through pitches. When I come north from spring training, I've always had that problem. Now I have problems with concentration. I can't get locked into the game. When I'm doing bad, doing well seems a thousand miles away. There is that very thin line to get back over, but you can't leap automatically.

No one is more aware of my failings than I am. The guys have been good to me. They have seen other players going bad. They try to treat me pretty much the same as they always have. Since I've been on the team for years, we have a closeness. Still, I just don't feel the same when I'm going real bad.

June 18.
Pirates beat the Cubs, 3–1.

June 19.
Pirates split a double-header with the Cubs and climb a half game out of the cellar. Stargell hits his nineteenth homer.

Joe Brown exonerates Bill Virdon from any blame for the recent bad play of the Piraes. "The manager has nothing to do with what happened. If there is any blame, it should go to me and the players. Maybe I had too much confidence in the club."

Brown says that the loss of Clemente has been a factor, but "we have other leaders on this club. Great players have stopped playing with other clubs and they have continued to win. The Yankees lost Ruth and Gehrig and won. They lost DiMaggio and won. I've heard people say we're supposed to have a dynasty in Pittsburg. You don't have a dynasty when you're in fifth place."

Brown tried to trade for a pitcher before the June 15 trading deadline. "I spoke to nine of the eleven clubs in our league. I made two clubs an offer and they decided against it.

June 20.
Chicago 5–Pittsburgh 3.

On this day last year, the Pirates were 36–25 and in first place by .005 percentage points.

June 21.
Pirates squeak by the Mets, 2–1.

The game is tied in the bottom of the ninth. The Pirates have the bases loaded and none out. Tug McGraw goes to a full count on Bob Robertson, who hits the next pitch on one hop to Felix Millan. Millan's throw to the plate forces out Clines, but the catcher's throw to first is so high that the right fielder catches it. He fires to Fregosi who tags out Al Oliver going to second. In the confusion, Dave Cash, who is on second base when the play starts, races to third base and home. Fregosi's frantic throw to the plate misses getting Cash by a step.

June 22.
Mets 5–Pirates 4.

The Pirates drop back to a cellar tie with the Phillies. Steve Blass lasts only one and two-thirds innings and is battered by five runs in the second.

June 23.
The Pirates beat the Mets 3–2 in ten innings.

June 24.
The Mets retaliate with a 5–2 victory. Stargell hits his twenty-second homer with the bases loaded. In the locker room during the third inning, infielder Fernando Gonzalez throws a temper tantrum when Gene Alley replaces Richie Hebner at third base. Gonzalez wanted to play, so he upsets the boxes on a table near the trainer's quarters and strews their contents on the floor. Next he hurls a stool in front of his locker.

June 25.
Pirates beat Montreal in a double header, 8–6, 3–1.

June 26.
Montreal destroys the Pirates, 10–3.

Blass, as a reliever, faces seventeen men in three and a third innings and nine reach base, four on walks and five on hits.

June 27.
St. Louis routs the Pirates 15–4.

Joe Brown is on a pitching hunt so he doesn't see this game at Three Rivers. Jim Rooker, in his first start, serves up back-to-back homers to Torre and Ted Simmons during a six-run third. When Blass comes in to mop up, he gives up one run in the seventh and four in the ninth.

Stargell says, "This must be the best last-place club you have ever seen. Don't worry about us. We'll get along."

June 28.
Pirates 6–St. Louis 0.

Stargell hits his twenty-third homer of the season and his three-hundredth career homer. The Pirates move out of the cellar.

June 29.
Pirates 4—Montreal 0.
This victory starts a five-game winning streak that lasts through July 2.

July 3.
St. Louis downs the Pirates in a double-header, 4–0, 7–6. Stargell hit a grand-slam homer, which tied the previous Pirate Club record set by Ralph Kiner. After the game, Willie wouldn't talk about his three hundred and first career homer. "Maybe in the winter I'll be able to look back on the homers, but I can't be impressed when we're losing. The team always comes first with me."

July 5.
Briles pitches nine innings to defeat the Cards 3–2.
Dal Maxvill, a shortstop released by Oakland, is considered for Pittsburgh. Gene Alley, Pirate shortstop, s,ays "I think we should get him." Alley is still woozy from Wednesday's heat. He has to be removed from the game when he almost faints in the dugout.

July 6 through 8.
The Pirates drop three games to the Dodgers.

July 9.
Day off. The Pirates are in fifth place, nine and a half games out, with a 37–44 record.
Maxvill joins the team in San Diego. Reliever Dave Giusti says: "The Cardinals could not have survived without Dal Maxvill." Nelson Briles, Maxvill's teammate in St. Louis in 1968 and 1969: "Maxie was a steadying influence on our infield in those successful years."

July 10.
Pirates defeat San Diego 4–3, snapping out of a three-game losing streak.
Gene Clines tears the ligaments in his right ankle, trying to steal from first to second and may be out for the rest of the season.

Dave Parker is called up from Charleston. Playing Double A ball in Salem in 1972, Parker hit .310 with twenty-two homers and a hundred one RBIs. In his first eighty-three games this season in Triple A, he batted .317 with nine homers and fifty-seven RBIs. Parker says: "A lot of people talk about me as being another Roberto Clemente or Willie Stargell. I just want to be known as Dave Parker."

July 11.
The Bucs beat San Diego again. Stargell hits number 25 and remarks that Dave Parker will break the Pirate home run-record in three years.
Briles is the winning pitcher. He leads the Pirates' staff with seven complete games. The rest of the Pirate starters have a combined total of nine complete games.

July 12.
Pirates 4—San Diego 0.
Stargell hits number 26. Pitcher Luke Walker lasts the entire game and allows only five hits, rarely goes to a three-ball count on a hitter and finishes with five strike outs and no walks.

July 13 through 15.
The Pirates lose two out of three games to the Giants and are pummeled 12–0 on Sunday.

July 16 through 18.
Back in Pittsburgh, the Dodgers take two out of three from the Pirates. In the last game of the series, Stargell hits number 28.
Richie Hebner is benched for two games because Virdon feels he is listening to the heckling of the fans and not paying enough attention to the game.

July 19.
Day off.

July 20.
The Pirates beat San Diego twice.
Stargell hits number 28, and second baseman Rennie Stennett goes seven for ten with two homers.

"If one of the umpires called a strike like you do,
you'd be in the dugout crying for a week."

*"Lean over that plate again, buddy!"*

**It is raining in Pittsburgh and Nelson
Briles, who is scheduled to pitch, waits for
the game to be called.**

Briles: We are just playing real bad baseball. I could have had three or four more wins, but we blew them.

I wish I was back in the mountains in California. They're fantastic outside of Reno, down into the Rockies and the Sierras. Dangerous territory with thousands of hidden lakes and wonderful fishing.

This is a dismal day. We've certainly had all the rain we need this year. Doesn't look like it's going to let up either. I thought we had a chance about one o'clock and then . . .

St. Louis sure has been playing good defensive ball. That's the way we won when I played there. Good defense and good pitching. That makes baseball. In St. Louis, we would fight and scrap and do any little thing to win. We have not been doing that in Pittsburgh this year. We have not been aggressive. We aren't that strong defensively, but we could go out there and be aggressive if anyone cared. We just haven't been fighting to win.

If we are rained out today, we'll put off the game until the end of the season. If the division title is in question, San Diego will come back and play. You'd be surprised. That game could be important.

**The game is called as the rain continues.
Jim Rooker talks in the damp dugout.**

Rooker: This is the best year I have ever had. The Pirates thought they were going to use me in long relief, and now I've got a good record as a starting pitcher. I'm as surprised as they are!

I am in better condition this year than I've ever been. I don't drink as much as I used to. My career means more and more to me, and I don't *have* to hit the bottle, so I've laid off. I enjoy a drink, but this year it's just been a glass of wine. After I pitch, I might have a bottle to relax. If you're on the road, there isn't much else to do. At night, you can't go back to the hotel and think about baseball every minute. When three or four guys get together,

it's easy to drink for hours and not even realize how much you've had while you sit around talking about baseball, politics and religion. If I am not on the road and come back to my home at ten in the morning, I tell my wife, "I didn't realize it was so late!"

When I played for Kansas City, I used to roam every city on road trips, but now the games mean much more to me, especially when we go to New York. We have had trouble with the Mets.

I have had trouble with crazy fans too. The other night, I was getting ready to take infield and this fan is standing there and says, "Fucker, where'd you learn to run bases?" I turn to look at this guy and think, "What's going on?" He's telling me about my crummy pitching. Now I go down to the third-base line for fly balls and the guy follows me in the stands. He has a friend with him. I've never had anybody get on me so bad. I got mad and said, "Okay, if you got something to say, come on out and say it." They were two big guys, bigger than me, but I told Bob Johnson, "You come on over here. If they come one at a time, all right. But not both of them at the same time. You make sure it's fair."

I said to the fans, "I'm coming half way and you come half way. We'll get this straightened out right here and now."

The guy says, "No, you come in the stands." I'm not allowed to do that, so I quit. The guy kept at me, so I went in the dugout. The game starts. In the second inning, I go down to the bullpen to throw a bit. This same fan leans over the rail and yells, "Rooker. Rooker's a prick." I tell him to let up. After I've thrown about two minutes, the fan comes down to the bullpen rail and says he wants to see me.

I said, "I've had enough." He was right where I could reach him.

He said, "You're a honky."

I casually said, "So what?"

Now he figured he wasn't aggravating me, so he said, "Really, you're okay. I like you."

Turns out these guys go around to every park in both leagues to see what kind of reaction they'll get from the players. They had just left Detroit and were on their way to Minnesota. I shook the guy's hand and said, "You got me good. Nobody ever got me this bad." It was a weird experience, but baseball has its own strange ways.

I have been in and out of the minors for thirteen years. My wife and I both love ball, so all the hardship hasn't bothered us. For a long time, we didn't have a home. We lived sometimes with her parents and sometimes with mine. It didn't matter, because we had baseball. I looked forward to coming to Pittsburgh this year, because they had been a winning club. Although 1973 has been a disaster for the team, I have finally gotten myself together. That's odd.

**Sunday, July 20th in the locker room.
Pittsburgh has just defeated San Diego in a
double header, 3-1 and 13-7. They are now
in third place in the NL East, 4 games out.**

Willie: You can't just come out and say what is going to happen. Every game is as important as the next one. If you go easily, the team that wins may win by a half a game. You can't relax and take anything for granted. A game lost today can cost you the pennant in September. We're going to have to play every game to win like today and then see what happens.

During the first half of the season, you find it hard to take each game seriously. Coming around the turn in the second half, we know we need all the consistency we can get. That is a combination of hitting, fielding, pitching, and good fundamental baseball. The last three or four ballgames have indicated that we are playing the type of ball we know we should be playing. Hopefully when we go into the second half in Chicago, we can continue. At least we're still in contention.

# A Party at the Stargells

# The All-Star Game

*Stargell going to the All-Star game*

*Bonds, Stargell, Mays*

*Stargell in the outfield in Kansas City*

*Hank Aaron and Stargell*

**Gayle shows up in a player's hotel room during the Pirates' series with the Mets on July 31.**

Gayle: I'm not just another baseball groupie. A groupie gets a screw and then gets kicked out of the room. I am friends with the players. I've been around baseball longer than most of them. When I was eleven years old, I hit a home run in the Polo Grounds. Willie Mays pitched to me and I had a real forty-ounce bat. I'm a slugger, but all I can throw is underhand.

The majority of groupies are between sixteen and nineteen, but I'm twenty-two. In Pittsburgh, all the girls are seventeen. There's this kid, Cindy, who I really love. She will phone and say, "Cincinnati's in town. Who should I call?" I'll be damned if I'll give her one of my men, so usually I tell her the name of one of the young ballplayers. I shouldn't be doing it, because she's a minor.

Cindy told me she had a conversation with another groupie, Carol. Cindy said, "Have you ever gotten anything from any of the players?" And Carol said, "No. They won't give me nothing. I once asked them for money, but they wouldn't give it to me." I wouldn't even ask for money. The guys just call, "Gayle, why don't you fly out here? Your ticket will be paid for." When I call the airlines, they'll say, "Oh, yeah, it's confirmed. Come on down." That's it. All summer I haven't spent a penny. Not one penny. I just pack up my suitcase whenever I have the urge and call somebody to send money for me to come.

I have been around the sports world too long to think of them as "Oh, professional athletes! They're something else!" They are not ballplayers to me. They're just men. I stick with them because I know what I'll get. I have never been treated wrong. Like one player from the Giants will play the Expos and then come to play the Mets and he will bring me a suitcase full of clothes from Montreal.

The presents I get—they make me feel real good. If I got money, I'd feel like a whore. This way, I feel I'm different. Sometimes I will answer the phone in a guy's room. I'll say I'm his wife. If a girl calls, he might say, "Come on up." For the majority of them, it's come and go. They really want someone special like me. I'm a friend, a Dear Abby. Everyone tells me their problems. I know more dirt than anybody else, and there aren't many females around who could say that.

Most ballplayers are like traveling salesmen. They're on the road, screwing everybody every night. They have an opportunity to have such an active sex life because of their fame. They could be the ugliest men in creation, but because they got a name for themselves, the girls will screw them, so ballplayers take advantage of girls in every city.

One time I had to call a pitcher in his room. I said, "Hey, whatcha doing?" He said, "I'm fucking this bitch." So I said, "What?" He said, "You heard me." All of a sudden a girl in the background says, "Get off the phone." I said, "I don't believe this." The guy goes, "Gayle, I'll talk to you later, after I get finished fucking this bitch."

That night the guy pitched. I had braided his hair for him in the afternoon. This black girl that was a complete dog comes up to me: "Are you the girl that pitcher was talking to this afternoon?" I said, "Yeah. Are you the bitch he was fucking?" She said, "Yeah. My name is Pia. Hi." I said, "Honey, I'm going to tell you something. If I was in bed with that man and he said that to another woman on the phone, he wouldn't be on the pitcher's mound, because he'd be cut from ear to ear." She said, "I don't mind."

"You're star struck, right?"

"Just as long as I can see him. Then I can go back and brag in school that I fucked a famous pitcher!"

Some ballplayers I won't have nothing to do with. Richie Hebner, I hate him. I ran into him in the hallway in the Essex House. Richie didn't know who I was or what I was doing there. He said, "Ooo, does she look good." I said, "Hey, look, you're not talking to one of the girls you meet in the street. And when you talk to me, you talk to me right." He said, "Well, look at this, hoo, hoo, hoo." I said, "That's right." I said, "When you want to talk to me, you gotta have respect, Hebner." He says, "You know my name?" I said, "Ugly as you are!" I got him so mad. So he said, "Oh, forget it." And every time we're together or he'll see me, he says, "Hi, Gayle how you doing? Are you all right?" 'Cause I shut him up good. That's why I don't like him, 'cause he's so stuck up.

I was outside the players' entrance in Pittsburgh and this girl had her tits hanging out. She said, "Aren't you Mrs. Milton?" I said, "Yes." She said, "I'm Ramon Fernandez's girlfriend." I said, "Honey, don't ever say that. I could be Mrs. Fernandez or her best friend." These girls don't have any class at all!

I have class, but in plain English, I'm a devil. That's what one outfielder calls me. Any girl can call that guy and ask to speak to him.

"Hi, my name is Carol."

"How're you doing, kid?"

"I'm alone. Are you busy?"

He'll say, "Not really. What you got in mind?"

"Could I come up?"

"Sure. I'm in Room 1516." That's it.

That outfielder will take anybody. He's crazy, but if you saw his wife, you'd know why he groans. Ugly is not the word for her. She's too demanding. She tells him when he can go out and when he can't.

I like that outfielder. When he left New York, I was supposed to go to Philly with him, but I decided not to. He called, "My roommate just got him a stewardess. When are you coming?" I told him I wasn't. He told his roommate, so I could hear on the phone, "Bring that other girl up for me."

I used to go with an infielder. I was sitting behind home plate at Shea Stadium and I looked at him standing there and my heart just flew to him. Literally flew. I couldn't think. A friend of his sat next to me at the game, so when I called the infielder I told him his friend had told me to call. I arranged to go to Pittsburgh. The Pirates had just come home from San Francisco. They got in at one-ten and my train pulled in at one-thirty. My man was at the station to meet me. We went straight to the hotel and checked in. He stayed with me that night.

The next day at the ballpark I heard his fiancé tell a player's wife, "My man didn't come home last night and when he came in this morning, he wouldn't give me any sex." So the player's wife says, "I don't care. My husband hasn't been home at all." I was two rows back and heard everything they said. Could you imagine what the other people thought? A couple of girls came over to me and said, "Did you hear what that guy's girlfriend and the player's wife were talking about?" I said, "Yeah." They couldn't believe it. They were shocked.

The infielder paid for me to be in Pittsburgh on my birthday. The American Legion was staying at the Pittsburgh Hilton and all those dirty old men were running around me when they found out I was alone. When the Padres got to town, I called one of them. "Look, these dirty old men are around knocking on my door. I can't even sleep." About an hour later, he knocked on my door and said, "Your bodyguard is here." We sat there watching TV and talking. If someone knocked on the door, he would answer. You know he is big. And black.

The next morning, my man called from the lobby and said he was on his way up. I told my bodyguard, "You better get out of here. Even though we didn't do nothing, that guy's going to think we did." They ran into each other in the elevator. Then I had all-out war with my guy. After that I watched them at games. My man wouldn't talk to him—even when he got to his base. That Friday night, my man asked what he could do for me. I said, "Baby, hit for me." He hit two home runs and went seven for ten in a double-header.

My ballplayers know I'm good luck. When one player's average went to two ninety-six, I got on the phone. The next day he was back at three hundred. On my birthday, I told them all: "You want to give me a birthday present? Hit me a home run." Five players. They all hit homers.

Ain't no way I talk to a player when he is in a bad mood. One night, a baseball friend was furious about not hitting. I made him stand in front of the mirror. His hands were too high on the bat. I told him to move them down. Then I said, "You've got to time your swing." He said, "You sound like my coach. Watch tomorrow night." He hit a homer and two doubles.

I'm weird that way. They get luck with me. That's why they hang around. I have baseball written in my head. I remember everything. You don't know the power I have over these guys.

Besides, I'm what everyone wants. My stomach may be a bit bigger than it's supposed to be, but basically I'm five two and the perfect weight is a hundred ten, which I am. I've got a tiny little waist—that's what I like most about myself. I'm not flat-chested. A ballplayer who I hadn't seen for a while said, "Where's your body been?" I said, "What'd you mean, my body?" He said, "I haven't seen your body around." That's the first thing anyone notices. Flash. See me. See my body. I exercise every day. I'm like the guys. They use their bodies all the time, too. They're conscious of their good shape, so they think about sex.

One day I was thinking about sex and called one guy. I got another. I'd never met him. When I said my name, he said, "Describe yourself." He said, "Just tell me. Were you in Pittsburgh last month?"

I said, "Yeah."

"Did you wear a pink halter and pink pants? And a red-white-and-blue halter and red pants?" He ran down every outfit I wore every day. That's when he was walking on crutches and he would see me sitting right behind home plate.

I say, "Yeah."

"Oh, I've been dying to meet you."

I said, "What?"

"I watched you every day. I didn't take my eyes off you." I couldn't believe it. It was really strange. So I went up to his room. Usually those guys have their girls together in the same room, but this man got a separate room for us.

He was . . . wow! I always get satisfied. If I'm not, I don't see the guy again. Take one outfielder in the American league. His wife is a doll. A sweetheart. His little girl is gorgeous, the apple of his eye. He doesn't run around that much. He keeps his business to himself. The first time I used amys (amyl nitrate) was with him. We both used them on the blanket. I got a feeling from the amys, but not from him. It's not what you have, it's how you use it. It can be thirteen inches and lousy. Or it can be two inches and good. If I don't get satisfied by someone, I don't go back. At least I should have an orgasm. That's why I don't see that outfielder any more.

A lot of guys will jump on you and be done. I like someone who takes time. I like to be with people that know me—we enjoy each other's com pany. I know how to satisfy him and he knows me. We enjoy being together. During the summer, I have sex at least once a day, but during the winter I do without it. I am not interested in players from other sports.

I would rather stick to the married ballplayers. They're not going to talk, because they don't know who'll tell their wives. A few players *do* talk to their wives. Once one wife finds out, she goes and tells another, so most married players are very cool. That's why I pick them.

Single players have a list a mile long. Most groupies want to get married, so they hit the single guys, go up to their rooms, and get screwed. They figure, "Maybe I'll get him if I go to bed with him." Of course, that's not the way. Sure, they get to bed. But that's the last the players think of them. Single players talk, too. "Hey, when you were in St. Louis, did you meet Lucy?" "In Pittsburgh, did you meet Carol?" Of all the people I've seen, nobody knows nothing, because every one of them has been married. Except the infielder. He has been married, but he's living with a girl, so he won't talk.

He is a funny person. He's hot and cold. He could be sitting and talking and be real nice. Then all of a sudden, he'll turn his head and . . . he's a Jekyll and Hyde. He's terrible. He gets me so mad. But then he's funny. He and Dock got their hair done in San Diego. He called and says, "Wait'll you see me when I get back." I said, "What do you mean?" He said, "Me and Dock got a process. My hair is slicked back." I said, "Oh, no." When I got off the train, I looked at his head and broke up. The next day Dock was wearing rollers. I said, "I don't believe these guys." My man let his hair grow back to normal, but Dock kept it up.

I prefer black guys because I was raised with black people in Floral Park, Brooklyn. I'm Jewish, but I went to an all-black school. My mother thinks my life is intriguing, because of the class of people I meet. She has had one man all her life and asks me questions about my sexual life constantly. Who's bigger, black or white? She drives me crazy. And she is prejudiced. Very prejudiced. She likes to cut up. Once she did it to a player when he called. He'd just gone from L.A. to San Diego by bus. My mother says, "What's you calling for at this hour?" The guy says, "I'm sorry. It's eleven here and I've just been thinking about Gayle on the whole bus trip and I had to call her." So my mother says, "Where're you from?" "Panama." "So you're a nigger, too?" My guy didn't take it. I took the phone from her and said, "Don't you mind her. She's prejudiced." But my guy still got angry. I've told everybody that she's sick. I say, "Be prepared. She'll say anything. Don't be shocked by the things that come out of her mouth." My guy just doesn't like the word "nigger."

My mother is still fascinated by my life. She said I should have been a prostitute, because I would have been the richest woman in the world!

**Willie, Gene Clines, and a girl in a hotel room after a night game against the Mets on August 1. The Pirates were defeated.**

Girl: I tell you, Willie Stargell, I know what I meant to cuss you out about. That purple passion. I went home and sit on the beanbag.

Willie: [*laughs*] The beanbag?

Girl: Why didn't you tell me what that drink was?

Willie: Whoa, whoa, whoa. I told you from that weekend.

Girl: Not the way you kept coming back fillin' up that blue glass. I had three a those big ole blue glasses. I woke up the next morning I didn't know what happened. That purple passion.

Willie: That wasn't purple passion. It was a depth charge.

Girl: It like to kilt me. That's beside the point, I don't have any papers. Give me something to roll me something in. This gonna be rolling in this. I don't have any papers. Shit, you can't smoke off that paper. It's too thick. My brother, I love you. Did you hear me hollerin' up there for you tonight? I was the *only* one. Me and about six little kids. I had on the Pirates' number seventeen and I was just jumping.

Willie: Is that right? I don't want you to get in no fight up there, 'cause these people in New York take the sport seriously.

Girl: I'm not thinkin' about those people. All I do is just jump out there with y'all. If it get too hot up there . . . God, there was another guard.

Clines: I said, "We need a fan!"

Willie: Come here a minute. I want to show you something.

Girl: 'Scuse me . . . that's how a lady says it!

Clines: I just felt kind of bad today about Vic Davallio getting traded. Especially in a game where you be around guys and playing with them for three or four years, you get almost attached to them. If they get hurt, it hurts you, too. Me and Vic now, we were tight. And when somethin' like that happens, what can I say to the guy? All I could do is wish him the best of luck. Check with you tomorrow, Will.

Willie: All right.

Girl: 'Bye, redneck.

Willie: [*reflecting*] Players can actually get to the verge of insanity. There are so many outstanding athletes I've run into that couldn't handle the game from a mental standpoint.

Number one, how you treat people is important. You've got to be able to get into a nasty situation and come out smelling like a rose. So many people are jealous that you're out there in the limelight. It looks like peaches and cream, but we're just like anyone else. We have different moods. Sometimes we're tired and our minds are exhausted. People want to talk about baseball all day. If you haven't been doing good, they want to give you some constructive criticism. Some just want to needle you. Players can actually become mad.

Our profession is different from the ordinary. We have to put on a show every night, and people want the big show. If I were good to the fans, I'd hit a hundred sixty-two home runs a year. We have to look exceptional. If I were a fan, I guess I'd expect the most too.

People don't go to a hundred sixty-two ballgames, but the game *they* see has to be the best. We've got to try to satisfy the fans. People can see when you're putting forth your every effort—that speaks for itself.

Do you have to answer to yourself or answer to the fans? This can be confusing to a ballplayer. A guy will go out and try to do his best. If he doesn't succeed, he gets booed. That booing has a way of sticking with some players and they get a real attitude. Fans should be sensitive, too.

**Bill Virdon relaxes in the morning in his
elegantly appointed hotel suite and
discusses the Pirates of 1973.**

Virdon: Managing is an interesting job, but when things are going rough, a manager has to take the blame. If I start criticizing the players, they're not going to be happy with me. They'll only get upset and hurt their performance. I make my own mistakes and I have my own problems. Like I don't know what to do about Steve Blass.

I have seen cases where a pitcher fell apart for a little while, but nothing like Steve. This is almost unbelievable, that a pitcher could lose everything. Steve has been wild in the bullpen at times, but he has also been in the bullpen and thrown strikes one right after the other. Just can't throw the ball over the plate in a game. He has no confidence in himself, he's lost all that. I have tried everything and nothing has worked.

It is possible that psychologically Steve doesn't want to play, but if that is the case, we are wasting our time. I wonder how much longer I can try to help. We would like to get him down to the minor leagues and pitch him, but we can't. The rule is that we have to put him on waivers, and when we did, other clubs claimed him. After all, he won nineteen games last year.

I try to be realistic. I say, "I got Blass, who has done so much for our game in the past. Just because he has a few bad outings, I can't say, 'The hell with him.' " I know Blass is physically all right. There is no reason why he can't pitch again. That isn't to say that he is ever going to, but I got to try to get him in a position where he can. I can't do that without being patient.

First I took his slider away; just let him throw a fast ball, curve ball. This is the way a pitcher starts when he first gets into pro ball: the only object is to throw the ball over the plate. A manager tries to concentrate on getting pitchers to rare back and get the ball down the middle. When they can get a fast ball over the plate, you work on a curve ball. Then you change to different pitches. Until the pitcher can throw the ball over the plate, you don't fool around with spot pitching. Young guys try to spot the ball outside and . . . ball one, ball two . . . Then they have to go right down the middle of the plate and somebody gets a hit!

Steve and I have looked at one hundred films from last year and this year. He pitched pretty good this spring, but now he rushes himself. That is why he's wild. He needs to hold his body back so his weight and arm come through at the same time. If he could slow down, he would get direction and power in his throw. If his body is out front and his arm's way back, he has to catch up with his arm. Then the ball flies out wild.

I can not tie a rope on Steve or hold him back when he gets started. If I knew *I* was rushing, I could correct myself to where I could throw the ball over the plate. Somehow Steve's got to take hold of himself and say, "This is

what I gotta do." I can't do it for him. Mel Wright can't do it for him. Steve has got to do it by himself.

Finally I will get to the point where I can't afford to tax the rest of the club by continuing to pitch Blass. I have got to decide where the breakoff point is. If we were having a year when everybody was playing well and pitching well, then we could handle the loss of Blass. But we are struggling as a team and Blass is just completely nothing.

We have had a lot of problems this year. In spring training, I put Zisk and Clines and May in a battle for position. I wasn't going to play somebody coming out of spring training that I could not justify by performance. Milt May did a real great job. He hit three twenty and a few home runs. Zisk and Clines had done nothing, so I have no regrets about starting the season with Milt May as catcher.

Sanguillan did a respectable job in the outfield, but I put him back as catcher, because we had won for three years with Sanguillan catching. He is a better catcher than Milt May. Nobody will argue that point. Milt knows that and so does everybody else. Manny's got experience, and knows the hitters better than Milt, because he has played longer.

Any pitcher's complaint about who is catching him is silly. It is not a good philosophy for a pitcher to rely on a catcher, because you don't know when a guy is going to break his finger and be out for two months. A pitcher should be a good pitcher if he's got Joe Blow catching.

We started out the season pretty good—won eight games and lost one, but any team can do that. Eventually the club went bad. I can't attribute it to Sanguillan's playing right field or Milt's catching, because we had a problem at shortstop and our pitchers weren't good. So I started trying to fill up some of the holes.

I like to fill my positions by juggling players. Cash can only play second base, although he has played third. If I want Cash in the lineup and Stennett too, I only got one choice. I have to move Stennett from second.

Stennett could end up playing anywhere. He could probably pitch if he wanted. He is just a great natural athlete. He does so many things well —unorthodox sometimes, but he gets the job done. No one knows for sure whether Rennie could be a good shortstop or not. He doesn't have the experience and he makes mistakes now, because he is at second base most of the time. A shortstop is involved in more plays, big plays that make a difference. Shortstop is not as tough as catching, but it's probably the most important position in the game.

We tried Jackie Hernandez at shortstop. I don't mean to be critical, because Jackie is a fine person, but after Jackie plays for a while, he gets careless and tries to hurry things. If he would do what his tools tell him, then he'd be a fine shortstop, but he tries to be better than himself. Real good

players read a situation and make the play. Jackie thinks he can get two outs when all he needs is one. Odds are, when you try to execute that quick, you are not even going to get one out. If Jackie would be Jackie, he would be a fine major-league shortstop. Jackie tries to be the best in the business; consequently he makes mistakes.

Alley is and has been one of the best shortstops. No question about it. He never got his feet on the ground this season. He has lost his confidence, doesn't have faith in his own tools. He worries, because he doesn't think he can move like he used to. We got Maxvill to cover at short for this season, but he's thirty-four and we have to plan. We might go out and trade for somebody, but a team should not fill holes by trading. A player should be brought up through your organization so you can train him and know him.

I like to have players that can fill a lot of different positions. If someone gets hurt, then I can throw anybody into the lineup and he has some experience. If you juggle players around, you don't mind giving one player a rest, because you know someone else is playing his position up to par. I only move Oliver because he is so capable. When I play him at first base, I'm not any worse off then I would be with Robertson. Of course, if you do your job well enough and hit good, you don't have to be moved. That's my answer. I don't even think about moving Stargell from left field.

Willie has got as great tools as anybody I've ever seen. When I first met him, he could run well, because he wasn't as heavy as he is now. He had good legs and a great arm. You could see he was going to be a good hitter. It wasn't any mystery that he'd make the major leagues.

Willie is a home-run hitter, but I do think he adjusts his swing to certain pitches. Sometimes he goes for the opposite field, and when a batter does that, he's not trying to hit home runs. If you are trying to hit the ball out of the park, you have a tendency to jerk and hit the ball to your power field, which would be right field for Will.

I think more of Willie than I do of anyone on the club. When I came back as a coach in '68 and '69, I worked with him in the outfield, but I have got to give him credit for the outfielder he's become. Because Willie is a power hitter, people forget that he is also an outstanding fielder.

Willie is as good a person as I've ever known. He is whiter than most whites. That's just a figure of speech, because I don't think of black and white. Will does things that a man should do, not what races should do. He is considerate and goes out of his way to help me. He tries to lead the club by his production and performance.

All my players aren't like Willie. Some are very selfish. Even if the club wins, if they've had a bad day, they can be very, very unhappy. I try to motivate these players to get them where they care for the team. Still, if that selfish player can produce every day, it's hard to say that he isn't helping the club, even though he doesn't help the atmosphere by being unhappy. Stargell is not that way. Willie Stargell wants to do well and has great pride in his ability and his performance, but if we win, that's all Willie needs. It works the other way too. Willie can go four for four, and if we lose, he is not happy. We have people in baseball that go four for four and if we lose ten in a row, they don't care.

This year I didn't want to put Willie in a bad position. His legs couldn't hold up in left field last year, so I moved him to first. In April, I found out that Will was actually pleased about going back to left field, because he's physically all right. Willie is a tough outfielder, who has learned his trade well. He is limited because of speed, but he catches most balls he gets to and his arm is good. He knows how to play the hitters and that is all there is to fielding the balls properly.

Willie has great control, which leads from his upbringing. His mother and father did a real fine job from what I could gather. I have seen Will close to flaring up when he was upset with a call, but he would never throw a bat or helmet, and he doesn't chew.

When Willie was coming up in the minors, I had been playing for seven or eight years. I enjoyed ball, even the last year I played, but I used to hate sitting around hotels, waiting and going to the park and hitting and then waiting for the game to start. It drove me batty, especially after I got older. I didn't mind that two and a half or three hours that you played, because I was concentrating. In the last year I played, I would catch myself during the game, sitting in the outfield with my mind wandering. I was only thirty-five years old when I quit. I could have continued to play for two or three years, but I wouldn't have played that well.

You got only one job when you're playing—to do *your* job. More things bother you as a manager. If you had all Stargells, you wouldn't need managers, but every player besides Will I have to worry about.

When you are a coach, you're not the one that raises hell. You get involved with the players and shoot the breeze with them. Maybe you go out and have a few drinks once in a while, if you don't make a habit of it. I did it, because I had played with a few of the guys not long before.

Managing is a lonely job. Players know you've got the whip and they steer clear. Guys do not do things naturally when you're around. I pretty well have the same nature as when I played. I try not to treat anyone different. I'm not one to constantly badger, but there's a certain amount of instruction I have to give. When somebody makes a mistake I ought to talk to the player. Not hollering at him or yelling or raising hell because he made a mistake. But immediately during the game or right after he does it, just call him over and tell him so he knows what he did and won't forget the next time. If I put it off till tomorrow, ten days later I forgot and he did it again.

I embarrass my players only on the rare occasions when I think they need embarrassing. I've sometimes wondered whether it was right. But when you've tried everything else and nothing works, sometimes you have to embarrass people. I make a large point of what I want—what should be done or what hasn't been done. In so many words. And they aren't friendly! Many times, guys get careless and say, "I did my best," which they didn't do. Then I have to wake them up. I call them in the office, not only for my benefit, but for theirs. I don't carry things to the press. The only reason the Hebner story has come out was because he came into my office and the writers were all in the room. I didn't ask him in. He came in. With Hebner, it's frustration, hypertension, and nerves. He wants to do well, but at times his concentration is nil. He has a temper and he lets it go. In the back of his mind he knows he just can't get himself together. It kills him.

Everything has been harder this year. Tempers have gotten away. We haven't been able to hit the tough pitchers like Twitchell and Seaver. That is where we miss Clemente more than anything, because he could hit the good pitchers. He hit them better than anybody else. Oliver can hit them maybe in the seventh inning, but Clemente would hit them right off. His steady bat set the tone for our other hitters.

We got big guys in the lineup who are swingers—they swing and miss a lot. They are not good hit-and-run men, with a few exceptions. Cash can hit and run. Sanguillan can hit and run. Oliver probably could, but he's not in a spot in the lineup where we really want him to. Now we've got Zisk and Robertson and Hebner. None of them run too well. They are always hitting with Stargell or one of the slower runners on base, so we can't play hit and run even if we wanted to.

Clines has not done anything for us all year. We didn't figure like he'd be here next year. In some cases, players get stagnant with one team. They are mad at the manager and general manager, because they aren't playing regularly. Everything is bad as far as they're concerned. If they go to a different club, they get themselves spruced up and do better.

There are so many elements to creating a team that wins. Most people don't realize more than they *see*. Suppose a guy bunts all the time or sacrifices himself to do his job. People think he's trying to get a hit and failing when a player is actually sacrificing his time at bat to get a man on base into scoring position.

Baseball is an interesting sport, because it is a team game where individual performance counts. What bothers me is the personalities of some of my fragile players. I do the best I can. If that's not enough, I can't help it. I like the money and the atmosphere of being in the big leagues, but I'm not going to ruin my health worrying about this job.

# Hall of Fame

*August 6.*
*The late Roberto Clemente is among six men inducted into the Baseball Hall of Fame today. The five-year waiting period was waived for Clemente, who died in an air crash last New Year's Eve off the coast of San Juan. Clemente was elected almost unanimously by a special vote of the nation's sportswriters this spring.*

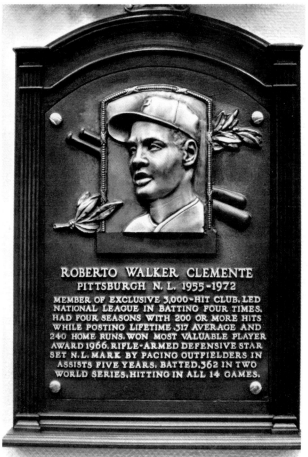

ROBERTO WALKER CLEMENTE
PITTSBURGH N.L. 1955-1972
MEMBER OF EXCLUSIVE 3,000-HIT CLUB. LED
NATIONAL LEAGUE IN BATTING FOUR TIMES.
HAD FOUR SEASONS WITH 200 OR MORE HITS
WHILE POSTING LIFETIME .317 AVERAGE AND
240 HOME RUNS. WON MOST VALUABLE PLAYER
AWARD 1966. RIFLE-ARMED DEFENSIVE STAR
SET N.L. MARK BY PACING OUTFIELDERS IN
ASSISTS FIVE YEARS. BATTED .362 IN TWO
WORLD SERIES, HITTING IN ALL 14 GAMES.

Willie: A couple of guys on the team came and asked me to hold a meeting for the players only. No coaches. I was to talk and stress the importance of our chance to win. I said no, because I didn't want anyone to think I was having a good year and trying to assume a role I had never assumed before. I felt it would be best if everyone on our team started to root for each other like we have done in the past.

I wanted the players to call a meeting collectively with no leader. Anyone could volunteer to air their problems out. Then one person could say, "Willie, what do you think?"

The guys felt the meeting would sound better coming from me. They wanted me to get on a podium and talk. I couldn't do that, so we didn't have the pep talk.

We started out all wrong this year. Any team's problems begin in the spring. If I had played first base, where I worked out in training, we would have really been off wrong! But now I look at all the mistakes that *were* made. We started with Milt May catching—something he had never done before. Sanguillan was our catcher when we won three division pennants and a World Series. He is a much better catcher than Milt May. If I had played first, Robertson would have been in left field, which is a position he can't handle. Sanguy started in right field where he had never played before. You may catch the ball, but it is not like catching!

Now you would have had two guys in the corners in the outfield that have no business being there, because outfield is the hardest position to play. It takes great concentration. Balls don't come to you often, but you must tell yourself that every pitch that is thrown is going to be a ball hit to you. Like a pilot, you have to check spots. If a plane is going to fly right, you have got to have instrument checks. Keep watching the wind, moving with the players, noticing whether the surface is wet or dry, if the grass is tall or short. How far are you from the fence? What is the fence made of? Can you be daring?

We went with Sanguy in right field. Abilitywise, he would have performed in the long run, but he lacked knowledge and made mental errors. In the first two months, Sanguy made nine actual errors. Trying to take a chance with players in important positions has got to hurt a team. And we have been hurt.

In the National League, every game makes a difference. Winning starts in spring training, in the exhibition games. You play like you have to win. I am not saying anyone is laying down on the job now, but it is easy to go back over the season and see where we lost games because the positions was all screwed up. Everybody was everywhere.

You could tell the guys' mental attitude from the clubhouse. All the guys are complaining. Early in the season, people criticized Milt May, saying he wasn't able to handle pitchers. Pitchers complain about the rotation, say they're not being given a chance to pitch. Clines wants to play every game.

Hebner doesn't like being platooned. Zisk doesn't say anything, but I know he wants to play every day.

Management has also gotten into a bind with the relief pitchers. During the first half of the season, it is good strategy to work relievers maybe once every third day. Because our pitching staff was not up to par, our best relievers, Giusti and Hernandez, had to pitch for the whole first half. Now when we need them going down the stretch, Giusti is exhausted and Ramon has a sore arm. We don't have no relief left.

We got a lot of unhappy guys on this ballclub. Sometimes we have to force the group situation together. Pittsburgh is a disturbed place, and the results show it. We have had a bad season.

Dear Willie:

I am an ardent Pirate fan who has attended better than sixty home games for the past ten seasons. Considering the team's recent performance, I need not explain in lengthy detail why I feel compelled to write this, my first letter to a PROFESSIONAL ATHLETE.

I am addressing this letter to you, Willie, because I know you have assumed leadership of the team in the absence of Roberto Clemente. Although I speak officially for only myself and a small group of equally ardent fans, I know my sentiments are unofficially representative of a growing number of fans. I, therefore, hope that this letter or its equivalent message finds its way to the Pirate clubhouse.

In the opinion of those for whom I am the official spokesman, the Pirates have shown an embarrassing lack of hustle, desire, and professional tenacity. Particularly during the past three weeks. We believe that as professional athletes you, more than anyone else, realize the worthless futility of trying to excuse this apparent condition by referring to anything other than your own performance, or as is presently the case, lack of it. From our vantage point in the stands, it often appears that the entire team is just going through the motions, each man singularly depicting his own version of the "I don't give a damm" attitude. I am certain I don't have to elaborate how this perception on the part of the fans works to curtail our interest, support, and finally attendance. It is difficult enough to support a team which is having trouble inconceivably inconsistent with the tremendous degree of talent which we still believe the Pirate possess. But, it becomes impossible to support such a team when, whether real or imagined, they appear to no longer CARE.

If, as you have said, the season is to be dedicated to the memory of the Great One, ROBERTO CLEMENTE, then we implore you, as professional athletes, to take seriously the name under which you have chosen to carry forth the "1973 CAMPAIGN" lest that name be besmirched by an admittedly less than professional performance. We are your fans and (as much as) we support you as professional athletes. But as your fans, we feel equally called upon to hold before your eyes the gleaming mirror of truth. (Perhaps hidden from your eyes by some unjustifiable sense of complacency) when your performance is undeniably less than profesional.

Whatever the source of trouble may be, we adjure you to take hold of the situation, to rekindle the professionalism of which we know you are capable, and to follow through on what we all desire:

"WIN THIS ONE FOR THE GREAT ONE"
A DISAPPOINTED PITTSBURGH FAN

**August 13.**
Pittsburgh 3—Cincinnati 2.

**August 14.**
Reds 5—Pirates 4.

**August 15.**
Reds 1—Pirates 0.

**August 16.**
Day off. Team reviews Pirates' batters for this season. Stargell is having his most consistent season. Zisk, since July 1, has delivered big blows. Six other players are below their lifetime averages:

|  | Lifetime | This season |
|---|---|---|
| Stennett | .306 | .246 |
| Cash | .290 | .264 |
| Al Oliver | .287 | .274 |
| Hebner | .291 | .268 |
| Sanguillan | .309 | .288 |
| Clines | .327 | .276 |

**August 17.**
Giants 5—Pirates 3.

**August 18.**
Pittsburgh 6—San Francisco 5.

**August 19.**
Pittsburgh 5—San Francisco 0.
The Pirates are now in second place, two games out. Jim Rooker pitches a five-hitter and contributes three singles to the 13-hit attack on the Giants.

**August 20.**
Houston 10—Pirates 2.
James Rodney Richard, six foot eight and twenty-three years old, hurls a two-hitter against the Pirates.

**August 21.**
Pittsburgh 6—Houston 3.

**August 22.**
Pirates 4—Astros 0.
Stargell is hit in the back of the neck by a Juan Pizarro pitch.

**August 23.**
Day off. Virdon says, "Win or lose the NL East race, there will be changes on the Pirates team make up next year. We need a top pitcher. We didn't trade this year, because it's not that easy to make trades. The other clubs want your left leg, an arm and a couple of other things in return for the pitcher you want. 1972 was a breeze. I was beginning to think there was nothing to this business of running a ballclub. I'm learning more about managing this year. I'm enjoying everything but losing."

**August 24.**
Atlanta 3—Pittsburgh 2.

**August 25.**
Pirates 6—Braves 5.
Richie Hebner leads off the 11th inning with his 18th home run to give the Pirates their victory.

**August 26.**
Atlanta 8—Pittsburgh 6.
The Pirates are a game and a half out of first.

**August 27.**
Day off.

**August 28.**
Pirates 8—Reds 3.

**August 29.**
Cincinnati 5—Pittsburgh 3.

**August 30.**
Day off. Virdon looks forward to a four game series with the Cubs without Dock Ellis, who has a sore right elbow, and Nelson Briles, who has an aching back. Stargell has persistent headaches, but continues to play. One sportswriter says, "Nobody will try to ignore pain more than Stargell. He is the Pete Rose type without wearing a neon sign in front of his baseball uniform."

# Hebner versus Virdon

## Pirate Spat: Everybody In the Dark

PITTSBURGH, Aug. 13 (UPI)—Joe L. Brown, general manager of the Pittsburgh Pirates, walked into a scheduled news conference at his office tonight just as two television lights blew out.

The cameramen were trying to repair the malfunction when Brown said: "You needn't bother with the lights —there'll be no press conference. I have no announcement to make. The reason for the announcement I was going to make is no longer necessary."

Brown then told newsmen, "Those of you who might speculate about a short meeting we had today—it had nothing to do with the reason for this press conference."

The statement surprised newsmen who had been summoned to the hastily called conference and had expected some comment on a heated verbal exchange between Manager Bill Virdon and his third baseman, Richie Hebner following the Pirates' 5-2 victory over the Atlanta Braves yesterday.

Hebner, angered because he was replaced at third base in the ninth inning by Gene Alley, began swearing loudly just when newsmen entered the clubhouse after the game.

Hebner walked into Virdon's office and asked why he had been taken out of the line-up. Virdon told him Alley was better defensively. Hebner then left the office and swore violently at Virdon.

Virdon went to Hebner, who was sitting at his locker and took objection to a two-word obscenity by the third baseman.

"Stand up and call me that," Virdon said.

Hebner refused.

"Get out of that chair and say that," Virdon repeated.

When Virdon challenged Hebner for the third time, the played did not budge.

"I've taken all I can from you!" Virdon shouted as he walked toward his office.

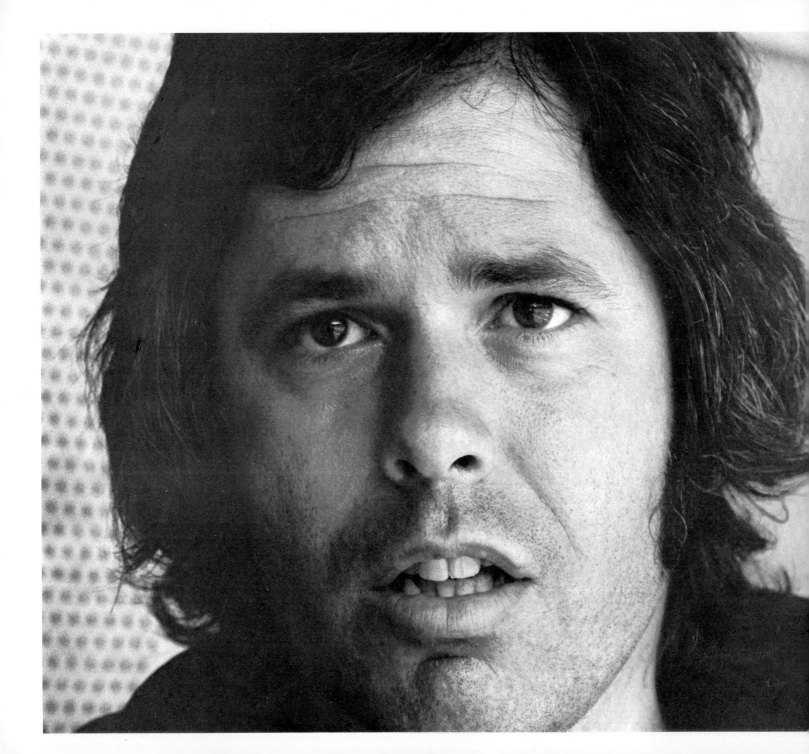

**Pitcher Nelson Briles talks before the game against Chicago.**

Briles: "What if all your errors were published in the newspaper every day like a baseball player's?" That's the clipping on our refrigerator at home.

Baseball is an individual game with individual statistics—good and bad, but you have to play as a team. If the hitters don't produce for me, it doesn't matter how well I pitch. I can still look bad because I lost the game. People look at cold figures, but statistics in baseball can be deceiving. A guy can be hitting two eighty, two ninety, but he never hits in the clutch or when it counts. A guy can be hitting two sixty, but all of his base hits counted. Who is more valuable to you? Which guy should get more money? And we are paid each year on what we did the previous year! If you don't have the statistics, you are not going to get that raise, because management can say, "You only did this—here—look at your statistics!"

You can pitch so well and come out defeated. Going to the end of the season last year, I was fourteen and eleven. My last three starts I got beat one–nothing, two–nothing, one–nothing; I gave up a total of four runs in three games. We should have won at least two out of those three. In one game, a Pirate didn't tag up on third base and was out. I was darn frustrated, especially because I am emotionally involved in the game.

Every pitch could mean winning or losing, so my concentration is very deep. I try to be cold and calloused in my approach, because I don't want anybody to know whether I'm hurt or tired or annoyed with the calls of the umpire. While I am on the field, I don't want anyone to read my mind, not even my teammates.

After the game, I can't let all that built-up emotion out by sitting in the clubhouse for forty-five minutes. Maybe other guys can, but I'm not programmed that way. I can't help carrying my feelings home, so they do affect my personal life. I can't forget overnight. I live with myself, but I am right back out there the next day. I don't brood.

You must really enjoy this profession; otherwise it becomes such day-to-day drudgery that you end up being no good to yourself or your club. I have always been on teams that were competing. Being successful contributes to the enjoyment of what you're doing, because if you're not successful, that's gotta be tough.

A player has to be very consistent, because the season is full of highs and lows. If you continually ride with them, that's exactly how your performance is going to be—high and low. A ballclub made of fluctuating individuals will not win, even if it has talent, because the game is based on percentages and consistency. They are most important.

Willie Stargell is consistent. If he has a great day, he is going to have the same attitude and approach the next day. If something bad happens to him, he is not going to get carried away with emotion and ride away. Willie is steady, not only in the way he plays the game, but also in the way he prepares himself.

I am very regimented in my pitching rotation with definite procedures between starts. We are on a five-man rotation, so if I pitch today, tomorrow I'll just play a little catch. Every morning, I'll do some running and exercises. The second day I throw for about ten minutes. If I have had problems with my breaking ball or not being able to move my fast ball, I might change them. In the final analysis, you're your own best coach, because coaches can perhaps see things you can't, but they aren't the ones who run, hit, field, or throw for you. The second day I do extra running to keep my legs good and strong, and the other two days I rest. From time to time I take ground balls on the infield, but basically I rest my arm.

The day before I pitch, I don't do anything. If we are on the road, I don't even go out. I try to concentrate and don't eat. Pitching is like going on stage with the butterflies and all. I would get very worried if I didn't have that nervousness. I would start to prepare myself better, because I would know that the adrenalin wasn't pumping. The day I pitch, I do some running, because I like to get the blood circulating and become acclimated to the local temperature. I want to get my body going and activate my mind.

I came from a poor family in Chico, California. Like in many small towns, athletics was the most important activity. My two older brothers played small-high-school athletics, so it was natural that they encouraged me.

I knew I was exceptional for the area, because I was throwing no-hitters. In junior high school and high school, sports were my identification. My friends weren't competitive, but we all wanted to do what we did well. Four of us had lettered in each sport every year; we also made the honor roll. A couple of guys signed baseball contracts and got big money, so I said, "Why shouldn't I?" I thought I was as good as anybody I had run across, but the money wasn't there for me. A scout said, "You're from a small town and you haven't pitched against the best competition in the state. We can't give you any money."

I graduated fifth in my class and could have gone to a lot of schools, but ended up at Santa Clara on an academic scholarship. All the athletic scholarships were gone. Our college was number one in the nation in baseball the year before I started. They had three undergraduate ballplayers sign, so they were afraid to pitch me when scouts came to the games. They thought I'd sign too.

I went away to summer ball in Canada and in three months I was sixteen and four—just having one helluva summer. All the scouts were there and one made a pitch to his ballclub: "This is how much we need to sign Briles.

Do we have it?" They said no. So he told me, "I'm out of the picture, but I know the major-league teams and I know the minor-league teams. Let's sit down and see where the best place for you to go is."

We decided on St. Louis, because their minor-league system did not have many promising young pitchers and their major-league pitching staff was old. The scout thought if I continued to show talent, I'd be in the majors in a hurry in the St. Louis organization. That was it. I signed with the Cardinals and a year later I was in the majors. I would probably have gone back to college for one more year except my father died in April of 1963 and, even though my mother was working, there was absolutely no money in the family. I had to work.

Pittsburgh was always trying to sign me, but they have never spent money on pitchers. Pittsburgh is primarily a hitting organization, although to me the most important ingredients in baseball are pitching and defense. That's why St. Louis wins. That's why the Dodgers win. (And because they learned not to beat themselves. They capitalize on the *other* team's mistakes!) Pittsburgh would sign guys that could hit, but if they needed pitchers, they traded for them. They got Giusti that way, they got me that way, they got Rooker that way. For the most part, the products of the Pirate farm system don't have a knowledge of pitching, a knowledge of the art. They can physically throw the ball, but if they can't think, they are not going to win. A pitcher has to have it all together all the time.

Changes in baseball—the artificial surfaces, lowering the mound and narrowing the strike zones, bringing the fences in—have all contributed to making pitching much more difficult. Pitchers have to adjust. Most of the time, we have our good stuff, but when we don't, the art of setting up hitters comes in: finessing here and there, trying to stay in the ballgame and keeping your glove to the ball. Maybe you can afford to let the man at bat hit a single, but you can't mess with a home run or an extra base hit.

A player is never going to become wealthy enough playing baseball not to work again. It's just not in the cards. In all the other professional sports, the attitude is: athletes have a short career, so they should get as much as they can. In baseball, management tries to say that love of ball is more important than money. That keeps the myth of purity going for the fans and also more money in the club's coffer. Consequently, the players in baseball don't get paid as much as other professional athletes.

There is nothing we can do about the reserve clause. Management makes a huge concession: If you've been in the major leagues ten years, and five with the same team, you get to approve a trade, but that covers five percent of the players. What kind of rule is that? What do we have?

I am a professional. I earn my living as a major-league baseball player, but I do not control my own career. An executive of a company has a right to take a more lucrative offer somewhere else, but we're tied down. It is ridiculous to call any discussions we have with our ownership "negotiation," because they've got all the hammers. In the final analysis, they can say: "Take it or leave it." If you leave it, you don't play and you don't get paid. That is the power of management. How can you negotiate when the general manager takes a strong line? Most of us are locked into a family and have responsibilities. We are not financially able to forget baseball.

Stan Musial was well liked in St. Louis, played there for a long time, and after his playing days were over, he was taken under the wing of Mr. Busch. Mr. Busch is in baseball because it is a tremendous write-off for his whole corporate set-up and a tremendous entrée for the beer business. He is a fan and likes to dabble, to be around athletes. When this Kurt Flood deal happened, it completely soured him. He considered that fight over the reserve clause to be a complete breakdown, because he is a man who both wants loyalty and gets it. He had a personal relationship with Flood—loaned him money and tried to help start him in business. After Flood turned against him, Busch didn't want to have anything to do with the club.

Most of the players, except the superstars, are going to be traded. When I played in St. Louis, I started a video-tape business, closed-circuit television on an industrial, commercial level. I designed systems for industry and schools. But I couldn't get any theater going in St. Louis. Two World Series back to back (1966 and 1967) and I still got no reaction. People weren't interested in ballplayers from St. Louis as a marketing possibility. When I was traded to Pittsburgh and we won the World Series in '71, a singer canceled out at the Holiday House and I heard about it. I said, "I'll go on," figuring I would have a couple of weeks to prepare. They called me on Wednesday when I got home and said, "You go on Sunday night." I said, "Let me get together with your people and we'll put a show together." She said, "You have one rehearsal." I sat down and knew I had to cover an hour. I had a couple of impressions and just thought of every song I could sing. When I got on stage, the whole planned format of the show fell right together. I took the playoffs and the World Series and wove songs in and out of stories. I made up one parody about the year when Baltimore was such a favorite, and Earl Weaver was played up so much, so I took, "Didn't We" and wrote, "This Time We Almost Beat Those Dirty Bucs" . . . and set it up by saying, "This is after the game and Frank Robinson and Earl Weaver are in the dugout:"

> This time we almost beat those dirty Bucs,
> Didn't we, Frank?
> This time we needed a kiss from Lady Luck,
> Didn't we, Frank?
> This time we had those Pirates right here
> in our hands,
> But they beat us and . . .

I have never really taken a concentrated study of voice, although I have sung in a lot of choirs and in singing groups. Holiday House wants me to come back for a third year now, but it depends on whether we get into the World Series or not.

Basically, some form of entertainment will be my future. I did weekend sports on television here in the winter of '71, which was a great experience. I learned how to read copy, how to read a teleprompter, and I did some of my own visuals for the show.

I have broader fields of interest than most ballplayers. After the game, guys go out and have a few drinks, do whatever they're going to, go back and sleep it off, get up, and go to the ballpark. I don't really hang around with the guys. I like to go to the theater and nightclubs, because I like to watch people work. I enjoy meeting entertainers and being with them. Most players don't have my background. In college, I was in arts and had a math major. I also studied physics, geometry, trigonometry, and did plays on top of my studies. I got a real education!

I have always looked to the end of my baseball career, because I have to. I don't want to die two deaths, like most professional athletes. My career is going to continue. I feel comfortable in the performing world. That's me.

**Last night, the Pirates beat the Cubs, 7-0. Willie hit number 36. Jim Rooker got his seventh win. This Saturday afternoon, Al Oliver talks about his season after taking batting practice.**

I have always wanted to be the best. Anything that I'm supposed to do, I can do well. I can become a superstar, because I really don't have no weaknesses. I am a disciplined athlete. I might sip some wine now and then, but that's it. I am a firm believer in my rest, which sometimes disappoints my wife! But I insist on being in condition.

At the start of the season, I set goals. In 1973, for example, my goal was twenty home runs and one hundred RBIs. From the financial standpoint, I wanted to have a year where I could push a hundred thousand dollars. I can still get those statistics, but I have not had a set position with the club.

To become a star, you have to be recognized in one position, like center field or first base. *I* can't say I won't play first base, because I can't say anything to management. I either have to take it or quit. The club can do what it wants to. They don't recognize that I put out more than anyone and benefit less.

Baseball is strictly business. In the minor leagues, it is more or less a fun game, but here it is no fun anymore. They have a certain amount of time for you to produce, and if you don't, they will put someone else in.

I've always been a winner and played on winning ballclubs. Now if I had said I would not go to first base, possibly the Pirates would have fallen flat on their face. The team was having problems like the Hebner and Virdon incidents. That's why I didn't complain. I was the guy that kept this ballclub together, because I did go to a different position when no other guy could be called on to do it in all-star fashion. I came through in the clutch. I drove in important RBIs. I got the key hits, but I never got recognition. I broke up two no-hitters in one week. I have never faded against a good pitcher. I've always been right there. Doesn't faze me at all. Every day, I know for a fact that when I step on that home plate, nine chances out of ten I'm going to hit that baseball someplace. I don't strike out much.

I am pretty disciplined at the plate, although I'm not a very selective hitter. I used to swing at everything, but the more years I play in the big leagues, the more selective I become. Still, any pitch that is thrown around the plate, I swing at.

As I understand it, Pittsburgh was one of the last towns to have a black ballplayer in the big leagues, but as a whole, the Pittsburgh fans have been good to me. I enjoy the limelight, there's no doubt about it. I have had a great career here, especially in hitting and producing runs. I would say eighty-five percent of Pittsburgh is in my corner at this moment.

I was given the image of being a bad guy, a guy who would tear your head off violently. Sure I threw helmets and knocked over a water cooler in 1969 in St. Louis, I don't deny that. But for three years, that's all the sportswriters could say about me. They never wrote about my production. This year, I have started getting some credit from the Pittsburgh press and it has spread from there. I have a national reputation.

Personally I have been through almost everything. My wife is all black, but real fair-skinned. When we were married, we received hate mail from people who thought a black man had married a white woman. I never judge a person by their color and, in fact, I hadn't paid attention to the black and white situation until I started playing pro ball down in the South. My best friends are white. I have always said, if people had my attitudes toward life, there would not be any problems in any country today. White or black, I could care less. If two people can get along, that's cool, because we are all human and we all have to lay down and die the same way. There is no reason to hate because of color.

Most black athletes talk about how people react to the racial situation. If I saw a white man with a black woman, I wouldn't look twice. I would just keep on walking, 'cause it is nothing to me. But some white people see it and they panic. They are showing me that a black person, basically, is not good enough; a black *man* is certainly not good enough for a white woman.

My wife and I walk downtown and people twist their necks off. We get a lot of hard stares. It's amazing. I used to be touchy, my temper would rise and I would be on the verge of saying, "Whatchoo looking at?" Now it's funny to me, but it is pitiful too. Probably by the time the world gets better on the black and white situation, I'll be dead and gone. That's how long I think it's going to take.

Life for me hasn't been easy, so I am very sensitive. The pressure started with the death of my mother and father, then coming to the big leagues, getting married to what most people thought was a white woman, and receiving hate mail. On the Pirates, it is always blacks fighting other blacks for a job. In other words, Hebner was at third and Robertson was at first. They weren't going to move for nobody. The only reason Robertson moved was because he wasn't hitting. If he had been hitting, he would have no competition over first. Politics. That's one of the reasons I don't enjoy the game like I used to. It has gotten political.

The good guys who mean well in life always suffer. You have got to be tough, and that is why I always respected and liked Clemente. Here's a guy who could do everything except hit home runs. But that wasn't what held him back from getting publicity; people in Pittsburgh did not like him. In the early 50's, they weren't used to black ballplayers. If you are black, society expects you to be quiet. Most blacks feel inferior to whites anyway. Society

doesn't like a proud black man, because it feels that black man thinks he is as good as anyone else. Clemente was a proud man. He was my type of individual. He was one guy who appreciated my abilities and knew what I had. If he had been a manager, he would have fought for me. He always told me, "Don't worry. Your time will come if you just stay there. I know what you're going through, because I've been through it myself." It made me feel good hearing him say that. Clemente did not change for the fans. Fans would have liked for him to keep his mouth shut, but he didn't. He was always for himself.

Clemente was the most underrated superstar around. My definition of superstar is not only being a star on the field but an all-around human being. Our job is off the field, too. I do a lot of work with youth. Kids look up to ballplayers and it is important for an older man to be associated with younger kids. I know, because I had to bring up a brother without a father. I'm on the board of the Big Brothers of America, I'm with the Boys Club and I'm on the board of the YMCA—this year I was their honorary chairman. Yesterday I found out they want to present an award to me for my services to the Big Brothers.

I wish you got some reward for playing baseball. It is such a tough game and nobody gets any credit. I still want to play ball or I would never have signed a pro contract.

I'll be glad when the season is over, because I haven't felt comfortable on the field. Last year, I was relaxed. I'm a natural ballplayer, but now I don't do what comes natural. I don't have the right rhythms at first base. Every time the ball comes to me, I wonder whether I will catch it. I have had to cover more ground in center field without Clemente. Everything has been hard, especially because management doesn't care about me. They think I can shuffle around. It burns me up.

Next year there is no way in the world I would play baseball without knowing that I am going to play one position. Before I go between the white lines, I'll get the amount of money I want and feel I deserve. If I don't, I will sit it out or try some other occupation. I am interested in the insurance business and I have had a few job offers. My main goal in life is for people to respect me, not as Al Oliver the ballplayer, but as Al Oliver the person. I have pride in myself. I am the only guy I know that never took advantage of anyone. I always stand up for what I feel is right, and I'm right in this case.

**Dave Ricketts is thirty-eight years old and started in basball as a catcher. For the past three years, he has been the Pirates' bullpen coach. He talks before pitching for batting practice.**

Ricketts: I am a bullpen coach. My job is to help people. I try to help catchers, and maybe some pitchers, but basically I react to situations. Like Clines went home and got sick last night. Got stomach cramps and had to go over to the hospital. Everything that happens to Stargell happens to Clines. Today I'll be all over Clines, teasing him in the clubhouse. It's funny and everybody gets a big kick out of it. If you can laugh at yourself, it is a funny world. The players are under such pressure that their only relief is through humor. With laughter they can get rid of any feelings of guilt or anger or frustration.

Guys do things you never think they would. Clines misjudged a fly ball and started to limp. He went over to the turf and patted it down. In baseball, when you do something wrong, you never make an excuse. Clines misjudged the ball, but he is telling us, the ballplayers, that he hurt his leg. It is the turf's fault that he missed that ball. Our mistakes are funny to us, to our little inner circle in the clubhouse. Other people wouldn't understand and wouldn't find them funny. But Clines has to laugh too, because all the other players are laughing. Tomorrow he'll be laughing at someone else's mistake.

This year we are not correcting our mistakes. We laugh about overthrowing baseballs, but the point of bringing that error up is to emphasize the incident and make sure it doesn't happen again. If Dave Cash throws the ball to the wrong base, I'll walk in and say, "Hey, Dave, you've been doing it all year—throwing the ball to the wrong base." It hits Dave in the mind and he says, "Hey, I've been throwing balls to the wrong base." We are joking, but we're also telling him to shape up.

I try to help the players relax. Gene Clines's nerves are so bad he doesn't know what to do. Just the day-in-and-day-out pressure. I say, "You been screaming and hollering. You put all this pressure on yourself." Clines asked if I thought he was wrong. I said, "That's purely up to you. You make your own decisions." When he comes to me, I can give him advice, but I can not make decisions for other people.

I told Gene, "Don't go through the papers on any gripes that you have. If you talk to a sportswriter and he prints your complaints, then Virdon will have to say something to you through the press. Go talk to Virdon man to man and get things straightened out." This is my whole philsophy. Ballplayers come to me and say, "What's going on here?" I say, "There is one person that can answer all your questions. The manager. Go see him. Don't be walking around mumbling behind somebody's back. And don't go screaming to the press."

Virdon has an open door. You can walk in and talk to him any time. For instance, you can ask what he expects of you. The best managers never ask ballplayers to do what they can't do. Virdon would never ask Willie Stargell to run. He would send Willie up there in the last of the ninth inning as a pinch-hitter to hit a home run, because Willie can do that. Managing involves knowing the ballplayers and giving them enough confidence so they will come to you when something disturbs them. This keeps the turmoil down on the club.

Some ballplayers are never going to be satisfied, no matter what you do for them. You can play them every day and they will always find a reason to complain. This is human nature. As a coach, my job is to help ballplayers and minimize any trouble that could be brewing between the ballplayer and the manager. I try to get the ballplayer directly to the manager. I don't speak on anything that is the manager's business.

Bill Virdon is a very frank person, a very honest man. But people don't like honesty. When we tell a person the truth and he doesn't want to hear it, it hurts. Bill tells a player facts in a nice way, but if a player keeps egging and egging, Bill can be very frank and blunt. When you are a leader and everybody is looking up to you, you don't kid about people's abilities. You don't kid about their mental lapses. You don't down a person in front of other people the way I do. This is demeaning, but I am accepted for it, because they give it to me too. "You're the worst coach that ever lived." "You don't know anything." If I started taking what they said serious, I wouldn't be able to kid. It goes both ways.

I ran into trouble with one guy who came into the clubhouse. I would kid him, saying he was prejudiced. The ballplayers all laughed. This guy told the manager what I had said, because he thought the ballplayers believed me. He didn't realize I was kidding.

I said, "Look, man. When you come in that clubhouse, we accept you as a friend. You're an object of anything that goes on. If we are laughing, we're going to laugh at you too. Now you went and told someone on me. I am at least coming to you as a man, the way you should have come to me. If you had said, 'Some of the guys are taking you serious and I wish you'd stop,' I would have stopped. But you didn't come to me." He apologized. I said, "I don't dislike you. I accept you as a friend, but I'm hurt. I would never go to your boss if you did something I didn't like."

I try not to joke about race, because we have a lot of black ballplayers, including me, and the ball club is not one-hundred-percent integrated. The players shouldn't sacrifice their jobs worrying about color. One player came up to Joe Brown and said, "You know you call me 'black boy'?" Brown said, "When it comes to ballplayers, I don't know any color." Still, race is a sensitive issue with the Pirate players.

Some ballplayers think they do not play regularly because of prejudice. I am not in a position to judge. I do know that I want my job because I'm good. I work as hard or harder than anyone else to keep my job. If I thought I was a token black, I would sit on the bench and loaf. Willie Stargell got his job, not because he is black, but because he is a good ballplayer. When I was an active player, I was always mad because I wasn't playing. I wanted to play. Then I started looking at the situation. If I hit thirty home runs and drove in a hundred runs and hit three hundred, I would be playing. I respect Clines's feeling. He is mad because he is not playing. But I also respect the people who run the club, because they're trying to make money. It is their decision that Clines doesn't help us win.

We haven't been winning this year, but the players have to take the blame because they are the ones that do the performing. Like actors on stage, if they don't come out with a good show, they can't blame nobody but themselves. When ballplayers realize this, they are better off. No sense going around saying, "This guy didn't help me." Nobody can help a hitter at the plate. If he is going to get a base hit, he has to swing the bat himself. Maybe a player is holding the bat too high, but when he is out there, it's him and that pitcher. There is no way in the world anyone else can help.

When you pitch a bad ballgame, the team should play behind you. The ball team has to be understanding. We are not perfect, but whenever you start blaming somebody else you are through yourself. When an error is made behind the pitcher, he can not worry about the error and forget his own job. Then he is going to be in more trouble. The other day, Briles got in trouble and Cash and Jackie got a great double play for him. They got Briles out of trouble. Why shouldn't Briles, when one of the ballplayers behind him makes an error, bear down a bit harder and get *him* off the hook?

Baseball turns into teamwork when you have to pick up ballplayers who have made mistakes. In a tough situation, if a guy makes a mistake and you hear someone say, "Pick me up!" then the guys are mentally pulling together. If you keep making little mistakes, one on top of the other, they may cost you three ball games in the course of the year and mean a million dollars to the ballclub. We have made more than our share of mistakes.

Over the years, Pittsburgh has been a hitter's team. We have not learned to function as a whole team. We don't hit and run or bunt. We have had adequate defense, but we've depended on our hitters to win. A team like St. Louis has to be a whole team, because there are no one or two men to slug them out of a jam. Pittsburgh is in trouble this summer, partly because we are not that big power team we used to be. Last year we would wait for someone to hit a home run. Now we have to use teamwork—to hit and run, to bunt more often. Playing together is not easy for our team, because we are spoiled. We haven't had to sacrifice fly and push guys slowly around the bases. It's taking us a while to adjust. You can't change from one system to another overnight. We may not make it in time.

Willie: I have more respect for Ricketts than any man on the ballclub. It goes deeper than intelligence in terms of the game. I admire the way he handles his situation at home. His son had several tumor operations when he was twelve. It was a form of cancer and the boy died. Dave took it right in stride and never brought that to the ballpark. He kept his sorrow where it should be kept, away from ball, at home. He never made a mess or looked for sympathy or cried on anybody's shoulder. He always put the team first. At his lowest moment, he would still advise a player who had problems. Dave Ricketts is a hell of a man.

Ask anybody on the ballclub. Dave is the hardest-working coach. He throws batting practice better than anybody, because he can tell you what you are doing wrong and what you need to work on. He throws according to your weaknesses and he throws consistently. Dave would come out at any time of day or night or morning and work with you. You could go to him at midnight and he would help.

Although Dave is truly valuable to the players, he never tells anything he knows about management, because he works for the Pirates and is paid by the club. He protects the trust that management puts in him. After spring training, Ricketts knew that Clines was going to be cut. Clines asked him, but Dave would never talk. If he had betrayed the ballclub, he would have betrayed himself.

Dave understands constructive criticism. If I screwed up yesterday, he would say jokingly, "You messed up." Now if the situation comes up again, I'll think about it, because Ricketts blasted it on my mind in such an intelligent way. Some players can't take the truth, but when it comes with Ricketts's humor and his laugh, it is not so hard to take. That is why our clubhouse has been a really good place to be. Because Dave related to us, we could all relate to each other. We always had a counselor.

Around this league, there is a spooky legend. If you have Ricketts as coach, you are going to wind up in the money, because Ricketts coaches on winning teams. I hope it's true this year.

# The Fall

**Danny Murtaugh joined the team in Philadelphia on September 7. The Pirates won as Murtaugh managed his first game of the season.**

Willie: Murtaugh held a meeting yesterday with the club. It was sweet and simple. He went over the hitters and said, "It's a big series and let's everybody go out and bust his butts." We didn't need a pep talk. That is not done in baseball any more. The player knows what he has to do, he knows the responsibility he has to himself and the team, so he goes out and does what he can. I look at it in this sense: everybody on the club have a family and they make decisions and do what they feel is best for the family. It is no different from going out to play baseball. If you "baseball" off it and put "job" on—they are the same. You perform to get a raise and you have to be consistent to move up in your profession, no matter what you do. They don't have cheer leaders in corporations.

Danny said he felt bad about Bill—as bad as anyone else in the room. Managers are supposed to manage men, to command respect, win pennants, and keep millions of people coming to the ball park. But many times managers are put in unfortunate predicaments. If they don't win, it's their fault. When they don't have enough to work with, they can't make chicken salad out of chicken shit.

The team was shocked when Virdon was fired. I should say surprised, because after being in the game for so long, you are not shocked anymore unless a tragedy comes. Baseball is a big business. A manager can survive as long as he has a winning team. When he is losing, management has other horses waiting in the corral. I thought the change was made because we lost three out of four in the St. Louis series. If we had split with the Cardinals, possibly there wouldn't have been a change.

After each game in the St. Louis series, I was physically and mentally exhausted. I was wound up too tight. When we lost, a reporter asked me, "How did you lose?" I said, "I don't know." I wasn't telling the real truth. We have not been playing good fundamental ball. If a guy is on second base and there are no outs and the guy doesn't hit the ball toward second, but instead hits it very hard to left field, the guy on second base cannot tag up and go to third. The batter has lost his time at bat and hasn't done anything for the team. If he had hit the ball toward right field, he would have a chance to get a base hit, and if he didn't, he sure would make it possible for the base runner to get to third. With one out, the next hitter comes to bat, hits the ball hard to left field, and you have a run coming in from third. The team benefits. We have not been playing team ball. The players let Bill Virdon down. The club has the talent, but we never played up to our best.

When I am playing beside someone, I am rooting for that guy, because baseball is a team effort. You can't count on someone else to do your job. I am expected to hit home runs and drive in runs. For me to do that, the hitter in front of me has got to get on base. Without him doing his job, it is difficult for me to do mine.

In 1971, every time I was up, we had a man on first and second. I had an opportunity to drive in a lot of runs, which we haven't did much of this year. Now I am leading off the inning many times. But if I get upset because there are no men on base for me to drive in, guys should get frustrated with me for striking out when the bases are loaded. We are a team and should not complain from an individual point of view. When you pitch a helluva ball game, you can only do as well as the team behind you. Many guys pitch outstanding games and it doesn't show in their won-lost column. The fans just look at records, so players have only each other to look to for support. Our sanity comes from team spirit. When that goes, your mind can drive you up a wall. You don't have time to recuperate like in football. After a Sunday football game, you have a week to deal with your problems. In baseball, we are right back on the field.

I would cut off the season two weeks on both sides. People don't come out to the park in April because of the chill. If it is too cold for the fans, you can imagine what it's like for us—miserable. April is the pitchers' time of year. On a cold night, a guy that is throwing good and hard will have the game in control. We get Seaver in the first part of the year and he just runs past us. He is working all the time, when we are sitting on the bench, our hands getting cold, muscles tightening. It's far between swings. If I had my way, every Monday would be off. Then we would have something to look forward to. The club gave us all those days off in August when they know September is the driving month. Now we have twenty-five games in the next twenty-four days.

The traveling is going to be fast. Sunday afternoon we leave St. Louis and play Monday and Tuesday in Pittsburgh. Wednesday, Thursday, and Friday night we play in New York. We leave New York Saturday morning instead of Friday night because of the curfew going into Canada. You can't go over the border after midnight, but they won't schedule an afternoon game Friday. Saturday, we go through customs and straight to the ballpark, take a shower, put on uniforms, and PLAY BALL!

When fans turn on the TV, they don't want to hear no excuses about, "Hey, these guys just got in, so they may not be as sharp today." They want you to go out and give that little extra. We can't say, "Hey, we're not playing today. It's just too tough." We have to keep pushing.

Richie Zisk: I am not flashy, but I get the job done. Gotta hit the ball hard. I have played baseball since I was tiny and I would like to have a dollar for every time I came to bat.

I grew up in Long Island and I didn't know what a hardball was. We played stickball in the streets off a stoop. The only baseball I knew was if my dad took me to a game. When I was nine or ten, we moved to Livingston, New Jersey, a pretty primitive town. Dad changed his job, because he thought we should grow up in the country. There was a good Little League club and I was introduced to playing. Here I was with a glove on my hand and somebody my own size, my own age, pitching at me with a hardball. I found I could do well. My dad never pushed, but he encouraged me. He's in seventh heaven right now. Anything I want to do he's behind me one hundred percent. It's nice to know that.

Dad is a frustrated ballplayer and he's living through me. He tried to make it to the majors before World War II and didn't. Now he's there with me on the field at bat. When I slide, he feels me scrape my knee.

Our house never was run on a schedule, because I was always at practice or a game; I was always playing ball. My mom made so many sacrifices. I had been told in high school that I possessed qualities no one else did. My mom must have sensed that, too. It was her dream to see me as a major-league ballplayer, but she never did. She died of cancer.

I have one younger brother: sixteen years old and bigger than I am, six foot, six. He's got everything I want—blond hair, blue eyes, and what I call Mr. Spock ears, kind of pointed like an elf. He's following in my footsteps in my shadow. They still remember Richie did this and Richie did that, why can't you do it? He is athletically inclined, but would rather fish and hunt and read than play baseball, which is fine if that's what he wants to do. He hits a good ball, but "When Richie was your age, he could hit one farther." Always some remark like that. He doesn't have the drive I had. He finds my dad a little hard to take, because Dad is so tied up emotionally with me. I told him, "Don't hesitate to call or write me if you have problems. If I can't help you, go to Dad."

I was a little less than—a LOT less than—adequate when I first started playing professional ball. I worked hard with Bill Virdon two spring trainings and I've improved a lot. I used to get a bad jump on the ball, because I was nervous. I'm still improving. Bill hit me ball after ball in the outfield. Got me so tired I couldn't stand it. He said, "If you can catch a ball when you're tired, you can catch a ball anytime." I have always been able to hit. Playing extra years in the minors helped make me an even better hitter. I worked on concentration, cutting down my strikeouts and putting the ball in play. In the minors, you play ball for three months then go to Instruction

League for another two and you're off for the winter. After that there's spring training for two and a half months. Then you go to Waterbury, Connecticut, for two and a half months, and when that's over you go to Instruction League again. It's a vicious cycle.

There's no money in the minor leagues. I was married, and making five hundred dollars a month! They can't afford to pay you down there. My value to management is what I do here, not what I did in Charleston or Waterbury. But the more I improved myself down there, the more dividends it paid up here.

When I first came up to Pittsburgh, my mail was mixed. Some nice letters said, "Don't get depressed. We know you can play or you wouldn't be up here." On the other side of the table was people that come to the ballpark once a week. The one day I play, I don't do well. They write, "What are you doing here, you bum?" Now the majority of my mail is favorable. "We're real proud of what you have done." "You helped keep us in the race."

I did a personal appearance the other day in an appliance store downtown, for a natural-gas company. I'm Polish and they made enough of my favorite meal for eight hundred people. I was there for two hours autographing pictures and talking to people. I had them try my meal, to show what natural gas can do for cooking! The fans were so nice, they surprised me. Some were critical of the team, but me, they said I was terrific.

I feel a little funny, because the man I replaced . . . how could anyone replace him? Clemente had a way of exciting people. When he'd catch a ball, people would get excited. Or when he threw a ball, or hit a single, there was something electric about him. When he came up, the Pittsburgh Pirates were not the power, the strength they are now. They were looking for a sparkplug, some high point of the season, and that was Clemente. I'll never be that kind of player, but I'm going to be solid.

I was hoping all this season for an opportunity to play, but the club seemed set without me. My options were up and I couldn't go back to the minor leagues without being purchased by another ballclub. I figured I would probably be with Pittsburgh, but Manny Sanguillan was moved to right field to give Milt May a chance to catch. Then things started happening. We weren't winning, and the defense was hurt by Manny being in the outfield. He's a great catcher, and that's where he belongs. They finally realized it and started making changes, but Richie Zisk still wasn't in the change. I was hurting because I felt I deserved a chance, having done well in the minor leagues. I have done everything they ever asked me to do. Then Gene finally got hurt, and that opened a bit of a door. Once I got my foot in it, I wasn't about to take it out.

During the season, we have messed up all the time. No telling how much we worked on sound fundamental baseball in spring training. It's simple, but basics are bobbled all the time. An outfielder has to make a clean pickup on the ball and he has to make a good throw to the cutoff man—one that's high enough to catch it and throw at the same time. When he throws, he has to turn without looking and throw through instinct. We can't seem to perform. I don't know why.

I know my own limitations, but I try to work around them. I've had cartilage operations in both knees, so I don't have the speed of a Gene Clines, a Rusty Baker, or a Willie Mays. There are balls I'm not going to get to, but anything I get to, I can catch. I have to know the hitters a little better than Gene or Ollie, who can run. I'll watch how the pitcher's pitching and if everybody's swinging late, I will play a little further over to compensate for this hitter. If I see everybody's pulling the ball, maybe I'll move over a step or two. Concentration! That was one thing that Bill Virdon drubbed into me. You may be out there for a hundred eighty pitches during the game, but only three are gonna come to you. You don't know which three, so you gotta be ready on a hundred eighty of them. And you can't be worried about fielding mistakes while you're at the plate, or striking out when you're in the outfield! They are two separate areas. You've *really* gotta concentrate!

I'm going to build up my upper-body strength over the winter. Not for bulk weight, but for strength. Two prime examples are Robertson and Willie. Robertson is tight through his chest. Willie is strong, but he's loose. That's come through years and years of swinging the bat. I talked to Willie and he told me some exercises for the muscles used in the swing. I'm a combination wrist, arm, and back hitter. I employ everything. Willie just snaps from the waist. Hebner is like Willie. He doesn't have to take that big turn around. I want to work on increasing my strength without becoming bulky and tight. I have gotten stronger through batting practice and playing. My wife noticed it in my back the other day. We were fooling around and she said I seemed stronger. I looked in the mirror and I could see.

One thing nice about being in the majors. I have a bit of money. We just bought a king-sized bed for our home. I have dreamed about that, too!

I have two problems. One is the press. The paper is always talking about how big I am and how I can't run. I said to a reporter, "You make those statements in the papers. Do you know how fast I can run?" The reporter says, "No." I said, "Do you know what the average is for sixty yards?" "No." I said, "Do you know I am about a second under the average for sixty? You didn't know that, did you? Next time you print something, come to me and find out. I'll answer your questions. Until that, the stuff you're printing is fiction." This happens in newspapers. I'll never talk to a reporter about someone else, because he would run to that person and tell on me. The reporter twists what I said up and then you have a feud going.

I do have a silent feud going with my other problem—Joe Brown. I have gotten a lot of promises from Brown, and I'm not stupid. I have every single one of those promises written on a piece of paper with Brown's signature. He hasn't filled one promise. I am going to keep quiet down the stretch, but when the season's over, we're going to have it out. I have talked to Whitey Lockman of the Chicago Cubs. I want to go to Chicago. I could hit forty home runs a year easily at Wrigley Field. I could build my career.

The life span of a big-league ballplayer is not that great. I can't play for twenty years. I can't play until I'm forty-four. Old age happens early to everyone on the field. You just try to push that date away as far as possible, but it keeps getting closer. Every day I play, I get older.

To get to the big leagues you have to have skill. You have also got to be lucky and be in the right place at the right time. Believe me, I know what it is to be on the bottom and now I know what it is to be on top. I'm going to do everything in my power to stay right here, because I know getting here does not necessarily mean you will stay. If I can't get what I want, I might go back and finish school next year. I was working on a B.S. in elementary education. I would like to be a teacher.

September 2.
Chicago 5–Pirates 3.

September 3.
Pirates 5–St. Louis 4.
St. Louis 8–Pirates 3.
The Pirates win the first game after an inside-the field-homer by Hebner in the 13th inning.

September 4 and 5.
The Pirates are downed twice by the Cardinals.

September 6.
With twenty-five games left in the season, Bill Virdon is fired at 4:30 P.M. Joe Brown calls this "the most difficult decision in my thirty-five years in baseball, but I feel we have reached a point where we could not win in 1973. I hope we can still win with Murtaugh."
Virdon says, "I guess the season is my fault."

September 8.
Pirates 5–Philadelphia 3.

September 9.
Philadelphia 8–Pirates 7.
The Pirates have a 7–1 lead going into the bottom of the seventh and blow the game. Stargell hits number 39.

September 10.
The Pirates win 11–3 over the Cubs and are now one-half game out of first place in the National League East. In the last four games, Stargell has hit nine singles, four doubles, and one homer. His batting average goes from .289 to .305.
Zisk goes five for six, but hits himself with his own bat in the seventh inning and has a badly swollen left shin.
Steve Blass will start tomorrow against the Cubs. Murtaugh says, "I would rather try Blass than go with a rookie. From what I hear, Blass has been throwing good in the bullpen. His control is much better than it was earlier."
Going into the game, Blass is 3–7 with an ERA of 10.40. "Let's see," says Blass, "tomorrow I'm supposed to be on that hump out there. Much of this year, I've thought that hump was used for drainage."

September 11.
Pirates beaten 2–0 by the Cubs.
Blass is beaten by Randy Hundley's home run with one out in the fifth, and the Cubs, on Dal Maxvill's error on a double-play ball and Billy William's sacrifice fly, score their second run later in the fifth. "Blass will start in St. Louis on Sunday, "Danny Murtaugh announces after the game. "He showed today that he can help us."
Cubs' manager, Whitey Lockman says, "It is obvious that Blass is still struggling." But Blass allows only two hits, walks five, and hits only one batter. In the first inning, he walks Rick Monday on four pitches and says later, "Here I go again," but forces himself back in his groove. Blass lasts for five innings and admits he is tired. "I haven't pitched that long since June first when I went six or seven against the Reds."
Zisk's left shin has swelled to the size of a golf ball and he will be out for a few days.
Stargell, batting .305, is asked if he is trying to overtake Pete Rose's batting crown. Willie cracks: "Whoever heard of a hippo beating a greyhound?"

September 12.
Pirates 4–2.
Robertson, back playing first base regularly under Murtaugh, hits a three-run homer. "Murtaugh knows me better than anyone in this organization. Getting a chance to play all the time is a big thing. When I first got back in the lineup, it felt like the first week of spring training."
Dock Ellis is still back in Pittsburgh with a sore arm. He will throw hard today and then tell Joe Brown how his right elbow feels. Danny Murtaugh hasn't given any indication that he will use Ellis if his arm is okay.

September 13.
The Pirates move into first place in the NL East, beating the Cubs, 6–1.
Leaving Chicago, the Pirate bus gets jammed in traffic on the way to the airport. Stargell leads the club in a soul community sing, with lyrics left over from a stag party.
On the way from the St. Louis airport to the hotel, Manny Sanguillan, who has removed his white leather boots, discovers they are missing.
"Where's my chew?" asks Manny in his Latin accent.
"Sangy, is it one chew or two chews you're looking

for?" Zisk chides. "Why would somebody take your chew?"

Sangy limps into the hotel with one boot missing.

September 14.
The Pirates defeat the Cards, 3–1.
In the first inning, Parker singles and Al Oliver is hit by a pitch. Stargell singles and Parker scores. Hebner hits a high fly for a run-scoring double. After Milt May is intentionally walked, Robertson singles to center. Stargell scores and Hebner, coming from second, is declared out for missing home plate in his headlong slide. Hebner yells at the call. Stargell tries to restrain him. The umpire's face is covered with tobacco juice and Hebner is thrown out of the game.

Virdon drives 275 miles from his home in Springfield, Missouri, to hold the traditional farewell meeting with the team. He tells them, "I enjoyed managing you. I wish you luck and hope you will become world champions this year."

September 15.
Pirates 7–St. Louis 4.

September 16.
The Cards win, 7–3.
Steve Blass wobbles through six innings. Ellis joins the team, but is not scheduled to pitch.

September 17.
Pirates 10–New York 3.
The Pirates are now out front by one and a half games in the NL East. Stargell bangs in four extra base hits, including his fortieth home-run. Hebner hits a home run right after Stargell in the third inning, the ninth time this season that the Pirates have hit back-to-back homers.

September 18.
New York 6–Pirates 5.
The Mets rally for five runs in the ninth.

September 19.
New York 7–Pirates 3.
The Bucs have lost three out of the last four and remain in first in the NL East by .5. Willie hits number 41 in the sixth.
Rennie Stennett injures his rib cage while swinging at a pitch. He will be out of the lineup for several days.

**Danny Murtaugh first joined the Pirate organization twenty-six years ago. This is his fourth stint as manager.**

Murtaugh: Every manager, once he takes the job, knows that there is one definite—he is going to get fired. Very few of us participate long enough to retire. I was fired in the minor leagues. You just hope you get it later better than sooner!

I don't know anything of what happened before I got here, because I was on the road scouting. The club didn't play as well as everyone had expected. We had lots of personality problems. Bill had maybe one or two fellows that did not play as well as they had done in the past. Together, it added up to his dismissal. Billy Virdon was just a victim of circumstances, which is part of being a manager.

I'm an organizational man. The reason I came back was friendship and gratitude. Joe Brown is probably the best friend I have. We've been together for a long, long time and the gratitude comes in because Joe picked me up when the Murtaugh family didn't have anything. Everything in the world I have today I owe to Joe and to the Pittsburgh Pirates. When I had a chance to show my gratitude by stepping into a certain situation, I didn't like it but I did it for the club.

Everybody knows I like managing, but had quit because of a heart condition. Last time I got sick, I made up my mind I wasn't going to walk around like a sick person or act sick. I have regulated my forms of recreation, but I haven't abolished it! I'm just talking about golf.

As calm as I try to make myself be, pressures crop up when I'm managing, and I can only take them so long before I realize I had better get out. If I had my own way and I was physically fit, I would manage for the next twenty years. That's the only place to be in baseball.

It has been very difficult for me to come in now. Even though I know the abilities of the boys, I don't know at this late stage who is really using his abilities. After being idle two years, you lose a little sharpness off your thinking. When you are swapping challenges with other managers, when you're trying to contemplate a game plan, what system you're going to use for a game, it's most difficult.

Baseball managers are not *all* stupid! We have game plans like football managers. Before each series, we have a meeting in the clubhouse. We go over the hitters on the opposing team—their weaknesses and their strengths. We figure out where the batters are going to hit most of the balls. The pitcher always sets up the meeting, because he is pitching the game and knows in what part of the plate he's going to throw the ball.

I stand there in that clubhouse and think about what we're going to do that night. I try to anticipate situations. I go over the entire roster of the other

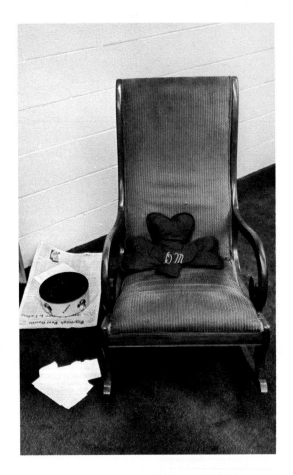

ballteams and figure out—maybe in the eighth or ninth inning, who would they use as a pinch-hitter? Who will I use as a pitcher? You turn it about to think what man on your team you want up there hitting in that certain situation and who is he going to hit against?

A manager plays men who are helping him to win the ballgame that particular day. Managers don't let men sit on the bench if they think they can help. My players may complain, but I like my athletes on the bench knowing that they are better than whoever is playing, because they feel like when they get in the ballgame, they're going to show me how wrong I was. Just remember, in order to maintain our job, we have to win. Those athletes out there, they know who is best on the club.

Managers have different ways of trying to win. When I manage, I like to get everybody in that ballgame as frequently as I can. In that way I always have them mentally and physically sharp in case I have to play them every day if one of my regulars gets hurt. Other managers, they like to go with a set lineup. You can't tell with managers.

I especially like seeing the young players come up. I'm instrumental in Zisk's being here. I was a super scout, a special-assignment man. I went up and saw him play in Parsippany, liked what I saw, and we drafted him. I want to see Zisk do well because all his life, Zisk wanted to be a major-league ballplayer. Now that he has made it and seen all these competitors fall by the wayside, it is almost too much of a shock. The percentage of anyone making the major-league level is pretty low. So even though Richie is a baby, agewise, he has learned about the facts of life, because he has been through more than most men.

Somewhere in the course of every American boy's life there is something he would like to be—maybe a doctor, maybe a lawyer, maybe a baseball player. Now all at once a baseball scout comes in and says, "Son, would you like to travel with my team?" This makes him important. If you don't have some kind of major-league ability, the scout won't approach you. So you have to go away and learn even more. If you fail, you can always say, "I tried out for the thing I wanted to do best of all and I wasn't good enough to make it, so therefore I am satisfied with my second choice of what I want to be." If you want it and you don't go out and try for baseball, no matter what you do, no matter what kind of a success you have made, still, back there in your mind you'll say, "Could I have made it had I gone away?" That is why you see so many boys trying to play baseball. Most fall by the wayside, but yet they do not regret it, because they tried the one thing they wanted to do.

I consider myself lucky. I'm fifty-six years old and I wanted to do one thing—be a baseball player. I made it. To me, inside, I consider myself a success, because I did the thing I wanted most of all to do.

I have watched Dave Parker since he's been with us, about four years. He has some good ability, but then the mental pressures come in. So many young fellows come up after they have been reading about these great pitchers, these great athletes, and now they find themselves hitting against them. The question is—can they mentally adjust?

In the minor leagues, selfish determination drives a player because he knows he has to do well to get into the majors. After getting to the majors, the greatest opportunity for staying with the ballclub is to have the ballclub win. Winning teams very rarely make wholesale changes. If you can help the ballclub win, you must have put a lot of your selfish traits away and then you're starting to become part of the team.

Years ago, we only had train rides and there was more time for togetherness. When I was young and breaking in, the object of the rookie was to get on the train first and run for the men's room, because that was where all the veterans would congregate. While they were telling stories, they were teaching the rookie a little bit about baseball night after night. The guys don't have time anymore. It's hard to learn team spirit now and that's a problem for the manager.

Athletes today are in better condition, bigger and stronger than the athletes of olden times, but I do not believe that the mental pressures were as great at the turn of the century as they are now. The world is speeding up and so are the life forms that athletes have to cope with. In the old days, you could probably play today and down there in California they wouldn't learn too much about the game until maybe the middle of next week. Before, if you made a mistake, nobody ever noticed it. Now when these boys make a mistake, the whole country reads about it.

Like when Willie got picked off first base in Philadelphia on September 7th. Because we won the game, everyone could laugh at Will, but that still lets Willie know he made a mistake. Willie knew he wasn't going to get any steal sign, but old Will had a sprinter's lead anyway. He wasn't going anywhere so he couldn't understand why he got picked off. If you're not going anywhere, you shouldn't get picked off. The other players kidded him. It's a way ballplayers have a lot of fun and get a message across at the same time. That's part of being an athlete. You match wits with the other team and your own teammates, as part of the great game.

Willie has assumed the role of team leader. When the going gets rough, he is going to take over the responsibilities of winning the ballgame for you. In the clubhouse, if you are having baseball problems or problems with your wife and family, instead of going to the manager, you call this guy over and talk to him. If someone calls you a nigger and you're black, or if you're white and a black man calls you some kind of real personal name, either the white or the black person will go to Willie and talk things over.

Willie has assumed the role of leader on the field, too. It's a matter of spirit—if you hit a high fly ball but yet when the ball is caught, you are down around second. The other night, Willie hit a ball into right center. The hit should have been a single and Will slipped into second on those legs of his for a double to set things up. This is showing the kids on the bench by the example of performance.

I was managing the Pirates when Willie came up. Down in Asheville, where he played for us, they had a fence in the outfield with a hill behind. Will used to hit the ball onto that hill. They used to call him, "On the Hill Will." He always had power, just had to learn to use it. Very tall, skinny black fellow. Could run. We were comparing his arm to Clemente's. That's the kind of arm and velocity Willie had. He was just a shade below Clemente when he came up.

Experience is a great teacher and Willie has learned through experience. I used to platoon him in the outfield against right- and left-handed pitching. Did that for a year. Then I found out that Willie could hit left-handed pitching and I left him in the ballgame. Now Willie, in his own way, has a pretty good knowledge of what just about every pitcher is going to throw. He has learned to play hitters. He has learned game situations. He's also learned to keep on an even keel, doesn't go up and down.

My theory is that you can't get a team up every day for one hundred sixty-two days. If I can get them even, I'm perfectly satisfied. I do not like being over jubilant in the clubhouse when we win nor overly sad when we lose. I think the emotions should be on an even keel instead of up and down, up and down. I don't think the human body can keep emotions like that and remain effective. In football you can do it, because you only play once a week. Baseball is every day.

Take Hebner, who is very highly emotional. That could be one of his problems. So many times he doesn't know what he has said until somebody tells him later. Richie is only a baby—twenty-four years old. One of these days, he is going to control his emotions and he will be great. Everyone is not capable of control, or emotionally alike, but I like my clubhouse with a quiet, unassuming confidence. I know that helps us win ballgames. I consider my ballplayers to be pros if they can accept victory or defeat in almost the same light. Then I am getting me a ballclub together.

The secret behind my managing is the fact that all the boys on my team know I believe in them and they will be given every opportunity to go good while they're going bad. I don't make snap judgments. But when I come in with twenty-five ballgames to play, I do not consider this my team. I still have to go along with the way they have been playing all summer. There is no way I can come in and make a complete turnabout in the strategies of the team. I don't have an opportunity to go with a lot of mistakes right off the bat, because I don't have the time. Time is running out this season.

I just try to manage the way I thought the club should have been run in the first place. I am trying to figure out how Bill was managing and my management will follow because we have been together so long. That's what makes the change easier for me. I am managing Bill's team, even though it's me managing.

I had no way of knowing Steve Blass's mental problem. I wasn't here. There's nothing physical about it. I have faith in human beings and the only thing I asked Blass was, "Do you think you've rested long enough?"

After you have been around so many people so many years, you realize what you can get from each individual unless they are completely through as an athlete. You have confidence in them and you *show* your confidence. My ballplayers know I am not a great conversationalist, but they also know that when I say something, it is important. I don't think the players are in too much of a position to question the whys and wheres of a manager.

I don't recall any racial friction on the club since I have been around. We were one of the first ballclubs to carry as many blacks as we have and we have been criticized. With the Pirates, if a black man and a white man had a quarrel, they just had a fist fight. We never assumed it was a racial riot. It was just two guys who had a disagreement. Two black men will have a fight and two white men will have a fight. Why not a black man and a white man in a baseball fight? They are both intense athletes striving for the same thing, with that strong desire. That's the only way they got where they are. Naturally tempers will explode between men playing ball. Race is not the explosive issue.

As long as I have ever managed, I have played the nine men that I thought were most capable of winning on a particular day, regardless of color. We fielded an all-black team against Philadelphia two years ago, and when Steve Blass and I were asked about it afterward, I brought out the fact that I didn't play nine black men or nine white men. To me, they were nine Pirates, so they played.

The color barrier is the lowest in the entertainment world. Baseball is part of that entertainment world. We realize that if you are good enough, you should be out there playing. You can't fool twenty-five athletes. They know who is best, although sometimes the best might not play because of the difficulties they might be having.

Right now I would say Giusti is in a pitching slump. A pitching slump by a reliever is magnified, because he is always right in the middle of every ballgame. It is up to him whether we are going to win or lose. They are overly important. The slightest mistake and naturally, he is the man responsible. A reliever gets only a third of an inning, or two-thirds, to show what he can do. He can go out there and have four bad two-thirds of an inning and we have lost four ball games. At this time of year, that hurts us.

David [Giusti] is in a situation where he just can't get untrapped. Little things happen—like bloop hits. We try to get our relief pitchers to make the batters hit the ball on the ground. To us, behind the scenes in baseball, the relief pitcher is supposed to come in and make the batter hit the ball on the ground no matter whether it's in the hole or not. Then he has done his job. When a reliever is going bad, the batter hits on the ground—but it is always in the hole. The ball the batter hits on the fist is always over the infielder's head. That good strike that you might need—the borderline strike—is called a ball by the umpire. Those little things magnify. Before you know it, you have a pitching slump from your reliever. These things are happening to Giusti right now, but he is still the best reliever in baseball and naturally he's going to play. Maybe he'll force me to use somebody else. We only have about ten days left.

Steve Blass: Giusti and I went to Play Street last night. I was drinking vodka and tonic and it's got me today, but at least Play Street is a safe bar to go to. My dad got rolled here a couple of years ago. This town scares the hell out of me.

I have roomed with Dave for three years now. He's a self-contained person who keeps a lot to himself. We don't talk much about pitching, but he has been there when *I've* had bad outings and we have gone for a few drinks. Now I'm doing the same for him. Dave's held the team together all season and he's just plain tired. Ever since Murtaugh's been back, Dave hasn't been able to pitch.

I was in a quandary when Virdon got fired. I had one of my best years pitching for him. But I pitched well under Danny, too, so I was happy to see Danny come back. If they had fired Virdon at the end of the season because the Pirates had lost, I would have understood. But they fired a manager who had won. That's not fair. And if fairness is not the issue, what is?

The one thing you look for in a manager is a man you can depend on being the same way day in and day out, and there is nobody more consistent than Bill Virdon. That's what makes me so damn sad. They didn't give him a chance to fail. Look at me. I have made a mess of this year and I'm still here, partly because Bill backed me.

Maybe Brown felt that a change of managers would change the team's spirit. I hate to think that a player can't find the answer within himself, that he needs to be told. I feel disappointed that a manager can make that much

**173**

of a difference to ballplayers. That really means *we* got Bill Virdon fired.

People said I was Virdon's meal ticket and I failed. But I have tried and I can't let guilt get to me—on top of everything else. I did what I could for my own problems. I even offered to go down to the minors, but when they put me on waivers, other teams still wanted me. Virdon tried to get me out of my mess. We talked over drinks. He took away every fancy pitch I have and pretended that I had just come up. Look, I was a mystery to myself. How was someone else supposed to figure me out? You can't blame Bill for this strange condition that I have had.

After the game in Cooperstown, I think Virdon knew he wasn't going to use me, but I didn't know that. Virdon could have told me I was through for this year, but that probably wouldn't have made me feel too good. That's the only thing he could have done that he didn't.

The bullpen was like purgatory for me. I felt like going to hell. I hated it. Oh, I enjoyed being the right-field warm-up man. But I was pitching so bad. Down in the bullpen, I thought I had a chance of getting in the ballgame every day. In relief. I didn't feel like I was prepared to pitch. Every day you wait and wonder more. When you're out on the field, you are always playing to win the game. In the bullpen, you sit and watch for the game to go wrong. You know that you'll only pitch when the game starts to go bad for the pitcher. That's a horrible position to play from.

I have been programmed as a starting pitcher, with four days to prepare myself for pitching. Now when the bullpen phone would ring, I would think: "I don't have enough time." I'd panic. I never knew whether I was prepared to get ready that quick. You go down and throw and throw and throw. All of a sudden, you may be in the game. It's such a drastic change from having four days to get ready and to think exactly how everything's going to go along. It is an extremely different type of preparation. I was amazed, because I was so used to being in control. I loved pitching and being on top of the game. Now I was out of control, in every way.

When Danny took over here on Friday, he had his meeting with the club and then called me in his office. He said, "You are going to have the ball on Tuesday. I don't know what the hell's been going on, but you're going to pitch. Have you had enough rest?"

I had Saturday, Sunday, and Monday to think about that game. I was very apprehensive. I hadn't pitched to a live hitter in six weeks, but I had pitched the equivalent of one hundred sixty games in the bullpen. Before that, I had pitched only batting practice in Chicago the trip before last [July 26]. I just had to get used to the idea of throwing strikes before I could pitch to a hitter.

Looking back, I think it was good I had some pressure put on me to go out and pitch in a ballgame that meant something. Danny has a good understanding of human nature. We were struggling for the pennant and he put me in a game that counted. The responsibility helped me. I wasn't just expected to go in and mop up in a game. I was starting again!

I have never been so nervous before a game in my life. I must have gone to the bathroom twenty-five times. I died a thousand deaths that morning. Couldn't sit still. The wind was blowing in. I like it when the wind is blowing in in Chicago. Then it is a great park to pitch in, but it's horrendous when the wind's blowing out.

I walked five guys and it was frightening, but I felt that even if things went wrong, I was in control. I wasn't missing by that much—it was more a result of the six-week layoff. I was amazed that I could come back that quickly. It was a very happy day.

I called my wife from the locker room and told her: "I'm back." It is tough on a wife, because there's nothing she can do to get a man's game around. She has just got to wait in the background—helping in small ways.

I talked to my two boys during the summer. I'd say: "When are you going to help me get my curve ball back?" "When are you going to get me squared away?" "Have you seen my slider anywhere? I seem to have lost it." We had some fun with my problems.

I am real close to my family. My wife and I have tried to make the game fun—rather than a live-or-die situation. We try to keep a stabilized life for the kids and ourselves. Somebody told me the kids were getting ribbed this year in school, but they haven't said anything to me. I guess every ballplayer's kids are teased when their dad has a bad day, makes a crucial error, or loses the ballgame. If you make a mistake in baseball, it is flashed on the scoreboard, printed in newspapers, and announced on TV. A lot of people can hide their mistakes. We have to live with them.

My boys are aware that this hasn't been one of the happiest summers. We are going to have fun, but our life can't be ideal, like a plastic toy. My boys look to me as their dad more than as Steve Blass, baseball player, and we have tried to work at that. I have them around the clubhouse so they can see the other guys are regular, too. It is part of an education for them—learning that they're just guys, although they are special.

Christopher—the youngest boy, is really fascinated by baseball. He's a fanatic. He gets guys' autographs. Whenever we have company, he'll parade the kids around: "Willie, will you sign this for my friend Joe?"

We have tried to teach the boys that baseball is what I do for a living. It doesn't make me any more special than Danny Whiten's dad who lives down the street. Besides, the boys are real fans.

I have always been fascinated by baseball from the fans' point of view. Sometimes when I'm pitching the next day, I get excused and go and watch

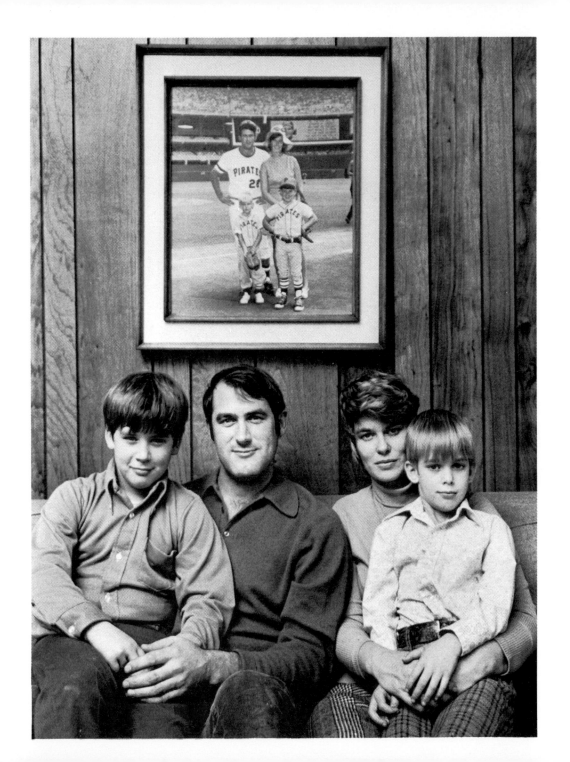

the game from the stands. It's like watching a different game. It looks mechanical, with everything in the right place. The game is very much in order. You don't have any idea of the emotion of the individual players. You are completely separated in the stands. You think the guys are robots —capable of performing at a consistent level all the time. The game is unreal from there. I sometimes wish that the game was as orderly down on the field as it seems from a seat in the stadium.

I like to pitch. I really enjoy it. I love the mental game of trying to set up a hitter. I take pleasure in getting hitters out. In a controlled situation like that, you can be very aggressive without hurting anyone. That's why I reacted to our instructions during spring training.

We had a meeting where a manager said that the pitchers were supposed to retaliate by hitting players on the opposing team if they were throwing at our batters. I got up and said I wouldn't: "If the batters don't like it, let them go out and punch the pitcher."

I don't like the theory behind retaliation. If a guy gets hit when he's at bat and he doesn't like it, he should go out and talk to the pitcher. But I know a pitcher has to back up his hitters, so it was silly of me to say no, because I didn't mean it. You have to throw at the batter. I have done it before, like when Reggie Cleveland hit a couple of our guys in St. Louis. Last year, the first ball I pitched to him brushed by his head. That was an obvious message: "Hey, that's it. We don't want any more guys hit." I came as close as I wanted. The message was received and acknowledged; he stopped throwing at our guys.

I will always remember one time when I didn't relatiate. Willie hit a home run off Bob Gibson two or three years ago in the first inning. The next time Willie came up, Gibson hit Willie right in the back. When Gibson came up to bat, I didn't brush him back or throw at him. I should have. It was a very obvious situation to me.

A player can tell whether a ball has just gotten away from a pitcher, or if he has hit someone deliberately. Sometimes a manager will say, "I want the first guy knocked on his ass," or "Wait till the pitcher comes up and get him." I have hit a lot of players this year, but for no purpose. I didn't get anything accomplished. I was just out of control.

Retaliation is standard practice and standard procedure, but it is hard for me to do, because I have a big psychological block. I would prefer never to have to brush back a hitter. I don't enjoy doing it, but we have to. All the responsibilities for getting back at the other team fall on the pitcher, who is the only one who has the weapon. He has to face everyone on the opposing team. There is an unwritten moral code that anything is excusable when you are playing hard, but when it goes beyond playing hard and you try to hurt somebody, then it is time to retaliate.

There is a ballplayer in the league who's notorious when he gets on first base. If someone hits a ground ball, he will go in and just tear up our second baseman or shortstop. He'll do anything he can to really nail them. There's no way for a second baseman or shortstop to get back at this guy, because he is an outfielder, so the pitcher has got to do it. I'm the one with the weapon. I just can't stand to hurt people.

This season has been so rough. I was used to Manny and it was strange not to have him catching me. When a guy has caught each one of us, he knows the patterns and the sequences we like to use. If you throw to one catcher enough, you are almost on the same wavelength. I almost balked in the game in St. Louis the other day, because Sanguy gave me a sign for a slider and I shook it off. I just knew he was going to go to a curve ball, but he went to a fast ball instead. I had almost started my motion for the curve, anticipating what his next move would be. They would have called it a balk.

I missed Sanguy until he started catching again, but at least he was around the clubhouse to have fun with. We have meetings when we go over the opposing hitters the first game of every series. Sanguy's locker is about three lockers away from mine. Whenever we get to McCovey or Billy Williams, Sanguy looks around, because he knows they frighten me. I get him by crawling further back in my locker when they start mentioning those names. I try to hide and Manny loves it.

We have had some classic meetings on the mound—Sanguy and me. The first year he came up, he was struggling with the language. He would come out to the mound—shuffling like it's his last step—take off his mask, look up at me and say, "Oh, you know," turn around, and leave. I had two or three guys on base and *I* didn't know at all. Not to this day. But Manny was satisfied and the manager thought Manny had taken care of the situation.

One day we were playing Atlanta. The bases were loaded and Aaron was at bat. Here comes Manny. He said, "Steve, you throw him and make him hit into a double play." He goes back and the next pitch Aaron hits up against the wall for a double and scores everybody. So Sanguy comes back and says, "You know, I say double play, not double!"

At least we still had Manny this year. Robbie [Clemente] and I had become very close, so that I really leaned on him. We had fun together in the clubhouse, but he meant more than that to me. He was the Pirates. Robbie had grown so much. He really kept up the spirit of the team—by the way he played, and by the way he helped everyone. Everything seemed out of order this year. Robbie was gone. Manny was not behind the plate. And I couldn't find my slider!

September 20.
Mets 4—Pirates 3.
The Pirates are still in first place by a half game. Mets
pull out a victory in the 13th inning. Dave Augustine hits
a ball that teeters on the fence and falls into an
outfielder's glove. It should have been a homer.
It could have been.

September 21.
New York 10—Pittsburgh 2.
Blass starts and is followed by five other pitchers.
Murtaugh uses twelve pitchers in two nights. The Mets
are now in first place.

September 22.
Rained out in Montreal.

September 23.
The Pirates beat Montreal twice, 6—3, 7—4 and trail the
Mets by a half game.

September 24.
The Pirates split a double-header with Montreal.

September 25.
The Pirates lose 2—1 to the Phillies. The Mets win.

September 26.
The Pirates trounce the Phillies 3—2. The Mets bow to the
Expos and their lead is cut to a half a game.

September 27.
The Pirates lose to the Phillies 3—2 in the 13th inning
and drop a full game behind the idle Mets.

September 28.
Montreal defeats Pittsburgh 3—2. The Mets game is
postponed due to rain.

Rennie Stennett: I got injured in New York, and in this game, when a person gets an injury, it takes a good while to get him back in. I could be playing now, but no one ever talked to me and I didn't talk to no one. I don't expect to get back in the lineup, because Dave Cash has been doing a good job.

I had been hitting good. Seems like every time things go well, some injury comes up and slows you down. Baseball is that way. Dave Augustine should have had a home run that Thursday in New York [September 20]. The ball hit some funny place on the fence and went right into the outfielder's glove. That was the real end of our season. You could tell someone was against us.

Like if Willie had not been slowed down in Houston [when he was hit in the head], he would have had about sixty home runs. Still, I don't see how anyone else can be the Most Valuable Player. Willie has home runs and RBIs and doubles and game-winning hits. But if the Pirates don't win, which they won't, that will give the writers an excuse not to give it to Stargell. I will be really disappointed. If Pete Rose wins, it will be bad for baseball. People would rather come to the stadium any day to see a home-run hitter rather than a singles hitter. Our team goes for power hitters, because they get the fans out to the stadium. The team thinks I can only get singles, but I am going to show them I'm a power hitter.

**Dock Ellis is
the Pirates' clown.
His good humor and
jostling takes the
pressure off his
teammates during the
long season. Ellis is
a controversial figure,
because he is flamboyant
and often exaggerates.**

**In the dugout, Ellis
banters daily with
his teammates, and we
hear him, under the
stress of a season
of defeat, try to keep
their spirits up.**

**What follows is a
humorous put-on, one
of his typical
comic inventions.**

Dock Ellis: Management tried to punish me. After I had been out sick for three weeks and came back in St. Louis, they didn't let me pitch. I was ready. The team needed me, but Joe Brown wanted to spank me. Daddy was showing his little boy who was in control. All he did was punish the team. Can't get me, I am free. I'm not owned by the team. Fuck the contract. If I win, I can do what I want. They can't control me.

Management thought I wanted a vacation, but Virdon had said, the day before they fired him, "Stay back. See the doctor and work out." My arm was sore, because I have problems with my tendons, but they're under the impression that I didn't want to pitch for Virdon. I'll pitch for anyone. Virdon sure didn't know how to deal with me at all. He tried one time, but when we got into a discussion, I knew more about ball than he did. I know the way people work. He didn't, because he had been treated so nice all the time. He never figured that management would try to stick it to anyone. Just didn't know. But he knows now!

Virdon said good-bye to us in St. Louis. He told me, "It was fun for two years." Virdon used to say I should take the other guys into consideration. But I don't deal with other guys. I deal with me. One time, leaving New York to go to Philly, I didn't want to ride no bus. I told Virdon I rode too many buses. He said, "Well, it's going to cost you a hundred dollars." I said, "Okay." When I went to walk out of the office, he wanted to preach. I said, "Man, you can't preach to me." I pitch. I win. I'm free.

During spring training, Virdon fined me because I wouldn't stay in the barracks. Hundred dollars a day. I only stayed for two weeks. I told him, "I got to have a lady. I got to go. You ain't locking me up in here." Guys telling me to sneak out at night. Sneaking out, nothing doing—I'm gone. On the beach. In the hotels up and down the beach. I am twenty-eight years old. They can't lock me up in no room and tell me I gotta be in. They were trying to get me to come back because they don't want the other guys to do it. I am not worried about the other guys. "It's twenty-five guys." That's what they always say to me. "All right, it's twenty-five guys. You got to deal with each one individually," I told them.

Management is afraid to deal with Al Oliver because they taken the job from him. Oliver worked so hard on that center-field drive. How are you going to tell him to go to first, when you asked him to go to the outfield because Robertson couldn't play anyplace else? But Oliver is not at first base for nothing. Management gave him a verbal agreement, maybe even some cash on the spot. They are not going to be able to get him back at first next year unless they give him much more money. Al Oliver has so many high standards. He wants to portray an image: being super, super-style. But he's still a regular old dude.

The great white hope of the Pirates is gone. They've as good as traded Robertson. I hope it's in this league, where he will be an out man for us. If he goes to the American League, he will make them forget about Babe Ruth. Don't have overpowering pitchers in the American. Just dibby-dabs.

The fans come down on Hebner and he goes after them in the stands. They would hang him right now. When Virdon had his fight with Hebner, I heard him screaming, but I was going out the door. If I had been there, I would have participated. Virdon shouldn't have been messing with no ballplayers down the stretch.

Other players is something else. I don't know how they play all year and don't be themselves. Like they sign autographs. One year management had us in cages like monkeys. I told them I wasn't going in no cage to sign no autographs. No way. They fined me two hundred dollars every time I wouldn't go, but all they do is fine you. The guys, they are not themselves. They try to be, but always with a hint of fear—something that I can't put my finger on. If my teammates didn't play ball they would have a job someplace else. Maybe they are afraid they can't get another job.

Maury Wills showed me the way to do different things. Here's a man making ninety-five thousand and he does the same thing I do. Like he comes to the ballpark in shorts, sandals, and shit. I used to look at him. He would be there before everyone; he left after everyone. When I'd look around on the plane and he wasn't there, I said, "Wow." Then I found out he was making excuses, like he had an appearance. He was doing what I was doing, but then he would tell stories about it. I would never lie. I'd say, "I'm not going. I'll meet you there when I get there. I don't have to go now." I don't like to travel with these guys anyway. They ain't got no sense. Act crazy, spit on the plane.

I do what I want. Some days I won't even run. So I don't run, because I don't feel like it. Can't feel like running every day. It never bothered me about being in shape. I stay in shape.

Virdon didn't know what condition the ballplayers was in. The guys weren't playing that well, so he was trying to psych us. He can put on my pants, but he can't get in my head. That's me. Murtaugh made mistakes in the beginning, too. But now he doesn't fuck with my mind and analyze me.

Management wants to talk to me, but they better not say nothing. What can they say? They got a rule where the wives can't travel with the team. No way they can tell me I can't have nobody to travel with. They can fine me all the money they want. Most of the guys are scared to bring their wives on the road. I've seen some of those wives hiding sometimes, because they would fine them five hundred dollars. It's just money!

One thing management knows about and don't discuss is our little pick-me-ups. Whole team is on pills. I have taken about fifteen at one time. You just got to be able to control it. Only four guys on the team can. When they had the All Star game in Atlanta two years ago, the clubhouse guy made a statement to one of the ballplayers: "You guys drink as much coffee as the Pirates." Coffee is the kicker. Makes them Dexamils kick. We play a game in Atlanta and the team will go through five pots of coffee. From eleven forty-five when we hit, until game time about two fifteen. No other team besides the All Star team does it. It will be a hundred degrees and you don't drink coffee in one-hundred-degree weather, unless . . . But you just imagine what the Pirates are doing—and you know everyone wants to get hyped up for the All Star game, too! Management doesn't look because they think it helps the gate. Keeps us winning. Keeps the fans coming.

I always tried to win any way I could. That's my freedom. Learned to take the sweat off my forehead. Gaylord Perry showed me how. They say us black guys got better stuff for "sweat balls." One time the umpire was going to tell me to wipe it off, so I did it myself. I feel like I'm good enough that I don't have to do that anymore. Guys that do—they're in a situation where they are afraid. Can't get themselves together.

I have a wicked gleam in my eye. Used to hit guys just to hit them. For fun. Like to break their necks. I might not like the way a guy looks. One guy, I hit him in the leg and broke his wrist, too. I told him, "I'm gonna get you." They didn't know what was happening. If the umpire sees you, there's an automatic fifty-dollar fine for the pitcher and the manager. Next time it happens, you are both out of the game.

Once I hit a guy in the back for no reason. Then we got in a fight. I punched him in the face. The catcher grabbed him. When the catcher went down on him, he bit the catcher. I started stomping the guy. In fact, Buddy Woods was on the team then. Him and a guy on our team got in a fight and he was on *our* team. That's the only time I ever saw that.

They say I started a fight in Chicago two years ago. I was throwing inside on this guy. That was the way we used to get him out. I threw him and and he ducked down. So the next time I came to the plate, I saw Durocher signal the pitcher to hit me. I got close to the plate, and when the pitcher started warming up, I backed out of the batter's box. He threw the ball right where I was standing. I told the catcher, "If he hits me, I'm going to beat you in the head with the bat and kick his ass." The umpire heard me, and called Murtaugh and Durocher out. I told Durocher, "If he hits me, I'm gonna kill you too." But when he started hollering back and forth, that's when the teams charged on the field. Clemente and Blass had me up against the wall to keep me from fighting. The fans were beating me in the head with my helmet. That's the only team fight we have ever been in.

I could care less what the team does. Only my pitching days do I want to work. The rest of the time I don't have any interest in the game. It gets tiresome coming to the ballpark. One year I told them, like they do in high school, "I'm sick." First they told me to come in. I said, "Man, I got a crook in my neck. I can't drive."

They said, "Well, give us the directions to your house so we can come up there with a doctor." I said okay. I gave them directions to the house. If they had followed them, they would have ended up in Alaska. Then I took the phone off the hook and stayed home two more days.

I grew up with all these dudes, playing ball, in the minor leagues and all else. So they are like brothers. If I go somewhere else, I would be an outsider. I know I'd find people in another organization trying to find out about my mind. I would throw out a few things, put them off my track, and they wouldn't hassle me no more. They like me here, yeah. They were punishing me, but they also need me.

All they have to do is leave me alone. One of the first things they say is, "As a team, we can't let you do this." But you're not letting *me* do it. I'm going to do it anyway.

### Dock Ellis in the dugout.

Let's go, you troops. And there go the Pirates. They're ready. They're wired up. They got about four-hundred-fifty greenies out there on the field. Only two people out there without their greenies. The catcher—he's high off tobacco. And Richie Hebner—his mind is fucked up. Now we've got to stand up for this jitterbug national anthem. I would really like to know who wrote the national anthem. Not who they *say* wrote it. What it means and all that old shit. Probably the same dude who wrote the Bible. Same damn old fool. They don't know who it is. The New Testament. The Old Testament. My ass. Stay tuned for a commercial.

Parker says, "All the guys out there have their pants in their tight ass. Who's got the tight ass? They do. That means *we're* going to win."

But I say they scared. I'm glad I don't have to stand out there for the national anthem. I would have to put my hat on.

Sure is cold. Have to abide by the rules. I see Nelson Briles went to the front office again and asked for Milt May to catch him. Parker didn't know about that. There's a lot of things he didn't know about, but I am going to teach him.

"What I like about you is that you're an individual that's in this world to live up to your own expectations. Not anybody else's. That's what I dig about you the most. I'm serious." That's what Parker says. "I'm not bullshitting you," he tells me.

I know he's not. He is supposed to be serious. The field looks good. Briles says he is hurt. What the fuck is he out there for? Don't make no damn sense. Talk about he hurt. If he hurt, get the fuck off the mound. Shit. Don't make no goddamn sense. He's a business man all right. Fucking with my money! Bullshit. What he going to do? When he go to talk about contract, say, "I didn't miss a start." Fuck around, lose the game; anyone can do that shit. That's what I'm going to do next year. If I'm here. I'll lip that bullshit up there when I don't have nothing and my arm hurt.

Look at that left-handed peep-out-of-ass hitter. Coming inside. Look at that. Fast ball inside. Ain't got no business throwing the ball inside. Don't make no sense. Telling them his arm hurts and going out there to pitch. They're going to wait the whole game to get McKee ready. Fucked around there. Bullshitting. But he started. This is a start. He ain't missed no starts. All he had to do was let somebody know. Now we gotta wait for the rain —some more. It's a goddamn shame, I'm telling you. I'm ready to go home right now.

Scoop [Al Oliver] might as well come in. Dude gotta warm up. Sit down, rest hisself. Shit. Get Willie up off his feet. Going to take him twenty minutes to warm up. And look at them damn Montreal ballplayers. They're just thriving. Fairley, can't wait to get a bat up there. First time I ever threw him out was on two ball and no strikes—fast ball. He swing the same way —curve ball, he hit a ground ball.

Why didn't Briles tell the manager a while ago his arm was hurting? Now he can say for the whole season he started every game. He went out there and it hurt him on the first pitch.

Damn rain coming back down again. Don't make no sense. What ya say, Oliver? Let's call the game. Let's get out of here. Be in the bar by five thirty, be drunk by a quarter to six.

So Giusti says, "You don't give a fuck whether you are high or not."

I know that Giusti. He's butting in my conversation anyway, that busy dago. Looks like a nigger to me. A goddamn gorilla, with all that hair. Ever seen a man with as much hair on his head as on his back? That's a gorilla. And they call me a monkey. He's the monkey.

"Tell me about my lance," Giusti asks.

What kind of lance?

"It's big," Giusti brags.

I says, "But you can't do nothing with it though." Steady rain. Steady rain. It's pitiful. We've been out a long time—the way Roger's moving around looks like he came to the ballpark high.

Oliver is sitting on the bench now and says "Didn't you see him on the game of the week, against the Dodgers? We were in Cincinnati. It was an off day for us. Rogers did the same thing—jumping and fidgeting."

Like he's wired up. Didn't see that game though. Very wired up.

"That was one of the fucking vacations you took. Maybe you missed it." Somebody is talking about me being sick again.

"But you were out for four weeks."

"So what? We're stupid people, you know that," I says. I tried to get Giusti to sign a contract with me, but he was scared. We could go get a hundred thousand apiece.

"You take too many fucking vacations," Giusti says. But he scared. Got a yellow streak up and down his ass. Talking shit.

I am going to leave this club. See where they end up at. Wouldn't have no color whatsoever on the team.

Somebody better turn down that speed machine on that pitcher out there. They got it on ten when they should have it on three. Mess around out there and take some of them Canadian greenies. He'll peter out in the next inning if he gets through this one.

They finally walked Stargell. Bigg-ass Steve. Tough shit. Somebody better key him down. I ain't nobody's fool. I should be at home somewhere laying up in some flat.

Sanguy—get in the game. You can catch now Nelson Briles is gone. Sanguy's naked as a jaybird. Ain't got nothing on. Look at his bare arms. Didn't think he was going to play. More delay. This is the most delayed game ever.

Can't think about nothing but sex in the dugout. Parker tells me about meeting a girl. He says to the girl, "What we'll do is play cards. If you lose, you gotta down four glasses of wine, right? Dig this, we're playing cards and every time she lost, she drank a glass of wine. She drank about twenty-five glasses of wine. So we go to the bedroom and she went to the bathroom and fell asleep. I should have took a picture of that. She slept on the toilet. Didn't want to wake up."

Parker tells me he has a friend who wants to fuck my cousin. I say he could. That's what you're supposed to do with the little broads—pick them up and fall into bed with them—

Why don't you put a whole bag of sawdust down in the box, especially for Scoop? Sanguy's catching. The quickest hands in ball. He's quick inside. Ain't got no business playing ball in no mud no way!

Somebody's going to set that batter's little legs up. You watch, that little motherfucker—hits the ball every time he comes to the plate. I couldn't get the ball down for a strike and I tried to come in and hit him in the tail and hit him in the head every time, because he's so damn little—trying to get the ball down and in, because you've got to be down and in for a strike. I can't wait to pitch again. This is a merry-go-round ass game.

Second inning and six twenty-five . . . If it rain now, they'll call it . . . Gibson won . . . [*St. Louis game is announced on scoreboard*] . . . [*Gonzales comes to bat*] . . . Let's go, Zapata! . . . Over here, we've got high-pockets Dave Parker from Cincinnati sitting down beside Ringo Dave Augustine.

189

Horseshit Dave Giusti coming out. The saving pitcher from Mellon Bank—Dave Giusti, just come in and sit down right here . . .

See, when I was a little boy, if I'd been a bat boy I would have been a hell of a bat boy. Ain't nothing I'd miss. Is that music for lovers? [*Organ in the stadium*] They're going to eat him up the way they ate me up in San Diego. You know, I'll never forget that ass-kicking . . . the one San Diego gave me this year . . .

If we don't get some pitching next year—this crowd, that's all you'll see next year . . . (There are about three-thousand people in the stadium) . . .

There is so many fucking good-looking broads. I'll give you an example.

You've been to Rochester. You know those Rochester broads. They're all over the goddamn ballpark just waiting to be picked up. They started fooling around with two. This one broad was like the top of the International League—she was fucking everyone in sight. A baseball Mollie. We go to this real nice steak house to eat and who's sporting this goddamn low life bitch—Foor's got a suit on and clean as hell—she's got fucking two pounds of make-up and shit . . . Two *tons* of make-up . . . A whore? You can wine and dine a whore too. But no man in his right mind if he had the chance wouldn't jump in her shit. My thinking's like that. She brought it up first and that's no shit. She called me up one night—she had to fly out the next morning. The next night I saw her—down at the Quality Court, we did our thing . . . Montreal's free; get all the sex you want, when you want it . . . People take care of you . . . All them broads in Montreal—you don't even need a wake up call . . . Just tell them what time to call you . . . Let the phone ring ten times and back it up with about three more calls. Damn broads. Don't think about nothing but sex in the dugout. Never.

**In the locker room after Montreal has won on Saturday.**

Willie: That's gotta be one of the longest damn days I have *ever* spent!

Oliver: Yeah, that was terrible . . .

Willie: They had to make that money. They just had to get that game in so they could get that gate. It's a sellout tomorrow, because they're giving away something on fan-appreciation day. They said it might rain in Chicago. Can you imagine having another tomorrow like it was today? San Diego—they have a hold pattern . . . might have to come to Chicago.

Oliver: A team like that can be pretty nasty.

Willie: They won't be nasty.

Oliver: You know, nothing to lose, not really wantin' to come. They might just get it in their minds to hurt somebody, kick someboy's behind.

Willie: I know I'd be kinda mad. They've had a frustrated year and to have to fly all the way out for one game and then fly all the way back again. You know what the funny part about it is? People don't give a damn about how the ballplayers feel.

Oliver: I been knowing that all along. Since when does it matter what the ballplayers feel? It don't matter how wet it is in that outfield. You're gonna play if you gotta *wade* through that water! I've never heard of them calling a game because of the outfield, you know? Have you?

Willie: And that's where ninety percent of everything takes place.

Oliver: Sure!

Willie: I've got to get up first thing in the morning and come back out here. Ten. I'd rather stay in the clubhouse tomorrow. We're going to have fifty-thousand people here. It's always that way on the last day.

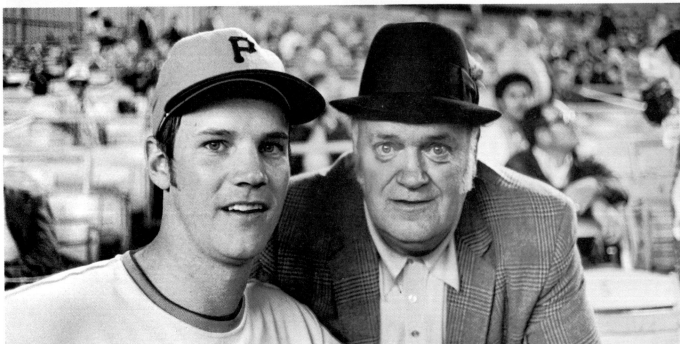

Briles: I'm going to go hunting this winter. Hunting falls in line with the nature of baseball, which is why ballplayers do it. We are very competitive on the field; then we are competitive with animals. We are also outdoorsy people. Most of us come from poor or relatively common families, raised in the Midwest or in the hills. Our older brothers have gone hunting, our fathers and grandfathers. It's a family legacy—like baseball.

When I was younger, I didn't hunt at all, because I was so busy playing ball. But now, it is the best R and R I could do. Maz [Bill Mazerowski] and I take our trail bikes, go way back up in the woods and hunt squirrels. Even though I am far removed from the rest of my family in California, I remain part of them through hunting.

Baseball is part of my heritage, too. Every boy dreams about playing professional ball. That dream may pass away one night, but it stays in your memory. Baseball is the first game you play with your father. When you have a son, you teach him to play ball so that he can dream for a while, too. Fathers and sons share a common experience. I remember the smell of fresh grass and the sun and the clean air. Now my boy comes down to the field and we have artificial turf and lights at night. You mostly smell stale hot dogs and phony grass, but the *idea* of baseball is still there. Baseball is an inheritance that's passed down from generation to generation.

I feel so strongly about the legacy of the game. Before I pitch, David [Brile's son] and I sit in the dugout and play catch. That is the nicest, most relaxed way for me to prepare a game. I forget the tensions of the mound. I think of my own childhood. I think of David beginning to grow up. It is the one gift I can give him.

193

Things have not changed since Murtaugh came back. We played well for a week, but the ability and the way you are playing over the long haul is going to show the type of club you are. We have gone back to the way we played all year—giving games away and making silly, dumb mistakes. That is exactly why we are the way we are—losing.

Clemente's death made a tremendous difference, because he carried a big load by producing consistently. Everything other guys used to do was gravy. They were the icing on the cake. Their runs didn't count in a situation; they just put the game out of reach. This year, those guys could not be the icing. They mean the game. The pressure is on them to produce in key situations time after time after time. That is a far greater mental discipline than having to produce when it doesn't count.

Some guys can drive in seventy runs which don't count. Maxvill in 1965 [when he was with the St. Louis Cardinals] got fifty RBIs, but they were phenomenal. We had guys that had lots more RBIs, but that year Maxvill drove in the biggest game-winning runs, even though he only hit two fifty.

We have had little pick-me-ups this year, but our level of consistency has been so low that we come all the way back down. You destroy the ups and end up with peaks and valleys. For the long haul of one hundred sixty-two games, you want to win ninety-five. The only way you're going to do that is play fundamental baseball. Not exceptional baseball. Fundamental baseball. Don't beat yourself.

Our young ballplayers are not schooled in the game. Mentally, they don't think about what has to be done on the field. They are not prepared for the game. It is so easy to beat ourselves: running bases, physical errors, throwing balls away, mental errors. We have run ourselves into the ground.

As soon as the season's over, I am going to record a novelty tune. It's called, "Hank, Please Don't Hit It off Me." It has a nice hook to it and the bridge is very good.

> Hey, Hank, I know you're going to do it,
> But please don't hit it off me.
> Hey, Hank, I've got a reputation
> And I've got a family . . .
> Please don't hit it,
> Please don't hit it off me.

The song is soft rock with a little country twist. Just a little flavor.

**Nelson Briles will not face Aaron in 1974.
He was traded to Kansas City in November.**

**The Pirates finally defeat Montreal on
Sunday afternoon, with their star pitcher
Jim Rooker getting the win. On Monday,
they wait in the clubhouse for the
player who brings the greenies. The mad
race in the Easter Division has brought
San Diego back to Pittsburgh to make up
a rained-out game.**

"Where is HE? Will somebody please call HIM. We've gotta do a respectable job!"

"Tell me something. If we win one, that's it. If the Mets lose two and we win and St. Louis is not raining and we go to St. Louis tomorrow. Then if we win in St. Louis, we go to New York?"

"Does that mean the loser tomorrow is in third place?"

"Give me an Excedrin when you throw questions like that! I can't figure out this division!"

"HE must be around here hiding. And all of us begging!"

"I've got five dollars HE won't make it on time. If Virdon was here, he'd scratch HIM from the lineup."

"What time did San Diego get in? Two or three? Where *are* the greenies?"

"The greenies—shit, that would do it right there."

"Where the hell is HE?"

"HE can't make it today."

"Big joke."

"No, HE called in and said HE couldn't make it."

"I'm on my way home if you can't find HIM."

"Fuck this shit."

"HE's an everyday hero, isn't HE?"

"If the Mets lose two, we go to St. Louis."

"All these fucking ifs, ifs, ifs."

"All we need is Carter's Little Liver Pills."

"We need a refueling."

"I'll tell you one thing. I can't trust that goddamn guy. I don't care what you tell HIM."

"Maybe HE thought it was a night game."

"They'll be digging me up from the grave."

"There's coffee in there."

"But what's it going to kick?"

"Maybe HE's talking to Joe Brown."

"HE might come in here popping and blow somebody's brains out."

"I hope nobody did a job on HIM."

**The player finally arrives.**

"Here HE is! Come on, sweetie. Get your ass over here."

"You are here!"

"Say, if you didn't come, I was going to quit."

"Ain't no way the Buccos could get ready without you, sweetie."

"We done quit, man!"

"Hey, I want two."

"Don't give him no greenies."

"No greenies for the big man."

"I've been on time the whole fucking year and the last day I'm late. But I do got the greenies."

**General relief that the greenies have arrived. Other players discuss a catch Al Oliver tried to make yesterday.**

Willie: Scoop, you gotta be the strongest man in the world.

Rennie: You would have caught the ball if you'd reached over in the stands.

Oliver: I wouldn't have caught it, because when I leaned over the railing, I only thought about the railing. I forgot about the ball!

Willie: I thought the guy from the stands blocked you. Do you see what time it is?

Oliver: Twelve-thirty. It might be thundering out there. We're expecting a flood at twelve-thirty.

Willie: Ain't no way the Mets are going to lose two. And St. Louis is home—doing nothing.

Oliver: Say it's four-thirty and the Mets win and we just walk off the field. That would be something.

Willie: Around the fourth inning, if the Mets win, we'll just stop playing.

Oliver: It's 2 to 2 in the eighth and Stargell's up. They announce that the Mets won and you leave the plate. You say, "Fuck you all. I'll save that for next year."

Willie: Can't be charging those rails, Scoop. I'm going to go out there and say hello to Nate Colbert. He'll probably kill me.

Oliver: [to Hebner] I had to put some ice on my hand before I went to bed.

Hebner: Let's see if you can do a skinny handle-fucking catch right there.

Willie: Hey, Giusti. Come out and throw a few palm balls.

A pitcher: Boys, I don't want to say anything, but here's the rundown for each month. April: 8–7; May: 13–14; June: 13–17; July: 17–13; August: 14–14; September: 15–16. If we win today, it will be 16–16.

Willie: But today's October!

**Cash to Zisk:** I think I'll be traded and go to Philadelphia. I'll probably hit two eighty playing every day. I don't know what's going on with our goddamn team. The one thing we need is a guy to get on base. I got into a slump and was taken out. I asked to play and I really got in the shithouse. But I said, "Come contract time and I'll really settle the situation. I no longer want to be with the club. I don't have any hard feelings about not playing, 'cause I know I should be out there. If I can't play, just be prepared to trade me someplace else." When you get so you can't play every day, you've gotta go.

Usually guys that bust their rear—they don't have much ability. They have to battle to make something of themselves. The guys that have ability—they don't give a fuck. Take a guy like Pete Rose. When he first came up, he didn't have anything. He battled and battled and made himself a great hitter. That's one way to do it. Like Kessinger, even though he can't hit. How many guys can get in the game and hit three hundred?

**Oliver walks by.**

**Cash:** Hey, I remember when you pulled that fucking water cooler off the wall in St. Louis. I said, "I'm not going to have anything to do with this motherfucker any more. I'm getting away from him."

**Oliver:** The water went everywhere. Like Niagara Falls. It's funny looking back on it, but at that time, I was in no mood to talk.

**Cash:** Remember the year Richie [Hebner] hit that brick wall?

**Oliver:** I wasn't there, but I heard about it. Richie broke his hand.

I've been thinking about changing the rules. I think if there's a man on second base and you hit the ball to the right to get the guy over, that should be a sacrifice.

**Cash:** That would be a tough one. Some guys hit to the right side automatically.

**Oliver:** But if you're unselfish and give up a time at bat to advance a guy, that's a sacrifice. The scorer is so far from the game, sitting in the press box on the third tier.

**Cash:** I think the official scorer should be down on the ground. That's what I feel strongly about.

**Dock:** We gotta play, guys. Because they sold the tickets to the fucking fans. We've got to play for the fucking fans. Boy, it's raining like a son of a gun. But the game must go on so we can go down in the mud.

Manny Sanguillan: I have a lot of trouble becoming a number one catcher in baseball because I am black and Spanish. I do have a good reputation around the Pirates, because I be ready when they need me. I did not want to go to right field, but I went. I was mad, but I didn't say anything. Since Clemente was Spanish, they wanted to play a Spanish player. Maybe I hit ten points higher in the outfield, but you see what they have—Richie Zisk, Gene Clines, Dave Parker. Richie Zisk—he have a lot of power, but he can not play left field because Willie is there. From 1970, people start to say they are going to move me to right field, because May is supposed to be the best catcher in baseball. That is what the sports writers say. I don't say he's not going to become a good catcher, but he has not got experience.

I feel better now catching, but I was moved too late. I never, never get in good shape. My balance was bad. I was throwing my ball with my right feet in the outfield and I fall down. My whole arm was wrong for catching.

When I tried coming back to catcher, it was too hard. Sometimes my body feel strong and I want to play, but the manager wouldn't use me. They asked me to come out and practice and I don't want to, but they wanted to use me because the ballclub was eleven games out of first place. We were supposed to be ten games out in first place with the great year Willie have and Scoop. People don't give Willie enough credit. After Clemente, Willie is the greatest ballplayer I have ever seen in my life. Clemente would tell me, "I've been watching Willie for many, many years and I'm so proud . . . all the routine plays he makes." Clemente was my hero all the way. Willie is my man now.

Willie was calling me the other day. "Why don't throw the ball higher?"

I say, "Willie, see, I don't have to. If I did, I would be out of balance."

Three days ago, Willie says, "Sanguy, I see you throw the ball good now."

I says, "Willie, that's the way I throw!" When I used to catch every day, Willie would tell Joe Morgan and Lou Brock, "Don't move. I bet on my man." Me! We have so much fun. The fun helps the team.

When I first came to the big leagues, I rented a room at the hotel. Willie used to ride me back and forth to the ballclub in the front seat of the car and talk to me in Spanish. We came so close friends. In '70, I tell him, "Willie, use my bat." He don't want to. In '71, he listened to me. In spring training, he didn't hit so many home runs, but he hit line drives. My bat really pays. Willie couldn't hit Niekro, the knuckleballer, because he was using a little, thin bat. Now Willie kills him with *my* bat.

Willie tells me he is happy to have met me and I give him ideas about bats. But Willie say: "You don't play no more winter ball, because every time you come back with a different bat and you drive me crazy trying to get

me to use that new bat." Maybe I'm particular, but I just like Willie.

We have a great pitching staff, but they were sick this year. Once Johnson was pitching and there was a man on first base and Johnson was letting the guy take a long lead. I go out to talk to him. I said, "Hey, this guy going to steal your base. You have to keep him close, otherwise forget it." Johnson says, "Save that shit for spring training." Spring training! The next pitch, the guy stole second and the game got tied. Maybe we could lost.

I go out to Dock and say, "Stop the man on first base." He says, "That's not my job. That's your job." But give *me* a chance.

Like sometimes I go in to tell Ramon, "Throw the ball overhand." And he throws it sidearm. We have a lot of fun. One day in St. Louis, a throw come home from left field. Walker is supposed to be behind home plate covering. He was right on the mound, and the guy was safe at home plate.

In Chicago the other day, Giusti was pitching. Someone hit a line drive. Willie was throwing in. I was yelling to Giusti, "Back me up. Back me up." He was between me and third base. The ball bounced and went behind me. I go down. I scream at Giusti, "You better get the next batter out!" He have to pitch if he don't play!

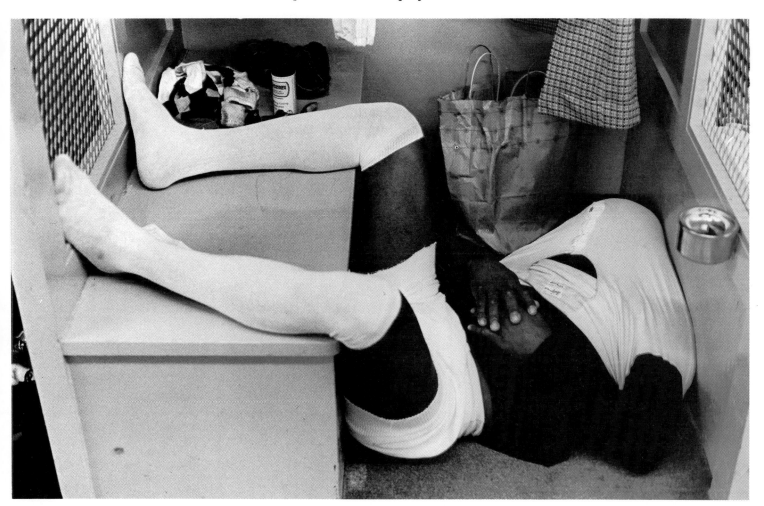

We need a left-handed pitcher. We need more fast runners. We have Parker and Clines, but we need more. When we lost the second game Saturday nobody knew how I run so fast. I can move quicker than anyone. They call me the road runner. All the time I be running. You don't see me stop. Beep, beep. I love to go. Roberto used to say I looked like an airplane with my arms like wings spread out. You watch me go from one to third. They call me the road runner, because every time I get extra bases. Yesterday, I came in so fast on Rooker's bunt.

At spring training, I knew we were going to have a rough time to win this year. I tell my wife. She thinks I'm cuckoo. She says, "How do you know?"

I say, "I know. Believe me. Maybe we not win. I can see the future."

My wife is sweet. She is one of the favorite ballplayer's wives. I met her in 1969 outside the old ballpark. I had just parked my car and see three girls coming down the hill. I go over and say, "Hi. You pretty." I ask her for her phone number, but she just laughed.

So I saw her in McKeesport in a restaurant where she worked. I asked for her phone number. She give me the first six numbers, but the last one was wrong. She said she really didn't know who I was. I don't go and tell someone, "I'm Manny Sanguillan." I just talk to people. Then she saw me on the ballfield and she used to wait for me every day outside. I used to ignore her. Finally, I let her go out with me.

We married in Puerto Rico in 1970 when I went to play baseball with Roberto. You have to give Clemente respect. You have to listen to what he says. You have to be close with people like Roberto and Willie. You learn something because that's the only way to become a good ballplayer.

When the season start in 1972, Virdon used to ask Willie a lot of questions, and Clemente. He used to talk to me, too, and he say, "You have to help me." But this year he stopped asking. I just start to like the man when they fired him. I don't think he was a bad man.

My number one manager is Danny, that's for sure. In '71, when we went into the play-offs, sometimes Danny helped me when I call different pitchers. He was my teacher in 1967 and '70 and '71. He said, "Now you have to show me what you know. We should win in the play-off and World Series." That was beautiful.

It is hard to keep each one happy, but that's what you have to try. Sometimes guys feel bad for one or two days. We have to learn to be aggressive of the self. In '72 in the All Star in Atlanta, we was losing three to two. I was the next hitter. A different manager make me bunt, but Danny let me hit. Yesterday, I take two bad pitches, then I got a hit. I was so happy for me, because I don't like walking.

I try to get along with everyone in baseball. I love to. We should have win all the way this year, but we can't win all the time.

I am not going to play winter ball now, because I only have one body and I can't afford to. I am going to spend more time with my baby, who will be two in November. When I bring him to the ballpark, we is really close. This winter I am going to stay in Pittsburgh, and speak in church where I am a minister. From there I am going to Panama to visit my parents.

**Dee Stargell and Donna Oliver are sitting in the stands while the Pirates play their last game against the San Diego Padres.**

Donna: The Mets just won. [Taking the division]

Dee: Oh, shit. No game tomorrow.

Donna: All of us should be crying.

Dee: It's a race for second place. Us and St. Louis.

Donna: If we win this game, we'll be tied for second.

Dee: What's second-place money?

Donna: About twelve hundred.

Dee: If we have to split with St. Louis, we'd probably do better to get third-place money.

Donna: Suppose they took the money from second- and third-place and split that. Third is seven hundred and fifty dollars.

Dee: That's not too bad.

Donna: When they take the taxes off, it's about a hundred dollars.

Dee: We'd go away on vacation! This is a lousy game to have to play. San Diego came all the way from California. That's three hundred sixty dollars a guy. Ten thousand dollars to bring them in for one day.

Donna: It's more than that with all the people they carry . . . the press . . . the organization. At least San Diego has some pitching.

Dee: We don't have any.

Donna: You have to give up someone in trade to get some pitching. They wouldn't.

204

Al told me, "If you lose, you deserve to lose." This ball club—we had the potential. I think if the club took eight people and said, "Here's your position," we would have a winning ballclub. But they've screwed around with Al, with Manny, and with Gene.

Dee: All spring they trained Willie for first base. The first day of the season, he went to left field. Make no mistake about it. Willie has *had* his.

Donna: But I don't think there's anyone on this ballclub that's had a worse shake than Al. They put him out there for two years. He's never played center field before. Now all of a sudden, it's first base. And it's been left and right field. It's one thing to switch him for a few months until he got comfortable. But not so many times in two years.

Dee: I don't know what's going to happen to us, but I don't think Willie's going to play in left field again.

Donna: But what's going to happen when Willie wants to come back to first base? Right now, Al's in an odd position. He's always had around a hundred RBIs, but he'll never get any recognition because people don't know where he is. Where is he? Center field. Or first base. When you identify a football player, it's with his position. I will say this for Al. He had a mild temperament to take this. Some of the others don't. I think they have messed Manny up to the point where he can't play.

Dee: That's a shame. They're just messing with all of them.

Donna: Manny doesn't complain, but he doesn't have the temperament. Deep down inside, it's eating away at him.

Dee: I guess they all feel that way in a new position.

Donna: Black players complain and they get penalized. When they moved Al back to first, he got hurt. It's his career and you only play for so many years.

Dee: It's pitiful.

Donna: It's disgusting. They're doing a good job of Dave Cash. I think if he were traded to another team and got the opportunity to play every day he'd say, "I'm going to show them." And he'll prove that he's a real good ballplayer. If Manny were traded, say, which I hope to God doesn't happen, his feelings might be so hurt that he couldn't play.

Dee: The Latin ballplayers are more loyal.

Donna: Blass hasn't made a contribution this year, but he's very grateful for being here. The whites don't fight for themselves.

Dee: Are you crazy?

Donna: No. Do you know why? Because every black player on this ballfield had to work three times as hard to get here. So they won't be pushed around.

Dee: I don't think the whites feel grateful.

Donna: I do. I'll give you an example. Hebner. He has his position. I don't think he has that deep down resentment, because he hasn't had to fight. He's nonchalant. He's pleased to be here.

Dee: Whites feel they're supposed to get it.

Donna: Black players as a whole don't drink like fishes. Don't stay out all night. Or mess around before they have to play. We know we *have* to be here. But white ballplayers do anything they want.

Dee: So that shows ungratefulness. They don't care.

Donna: It's nonchalance.

Dee: They know they're going to be here. I think Willie would agree with me. Sure Steve Blass is grateful.

Donna: But even when he was winning twenty games he was grateful.

Dee: He's a Joe Brown man. He's their man on the inside track. He figured if he did everything right, he'd have a job for later on. He's fattening up things for himself. For his interests.

Donna: He said that if it wasn't for the Pirates, he'd be in a small town being a farmer somewhere. Rather than thinking that he has a talent that he's selling. Even his wife tried to tell him: "Get what you can get while you are here." She's tough.

Dee: She was drinking—

Donna: Liquor talks. I believe that. White players don't see management as the enemy, 'cause they haven't had to fight like the black ballplayers.

Dee: [*Willie is at bat*] Come on, Willie. Do it now so we can be in second place. [*To Donna*] Be like Avis today, Number two. What a mess! We worked so hard. And look where we are.

Donna: That doesn't matter. White ballplayers get a position. They don't have to fight for it. There's no need for them to be resentful.

Dee: Blacks do have to really figure out what's going on to survive.

Donna: Like with Al. It's a pride thing. They said, "You're not good enough to play first base, 'cause this white guy can do it better." Robertson flops out, And they send Al out there for two years to learn a strange position and he learns it and the boy flops out, so Al comes back to first base. That's enough to insult anybody. I'd tell them they were out of their damn minds. I'll bet you next year there'll be six or seven people missing from this team. I hope it won't be us, being that we just bought a house. I wonder if all organizations are like this. So crazy.

Dee: Just about.

Donna: Except platooning. Pittsburgh has always had this thing about platooning. Al's philosophy is that he plays ball and he doesn't want anything else to do with them. If he needs money, he goes to the bank. If you take something from management, it puts you in a vulnerable position.

Dee: Third place!

Donna: I might get drunk tonight. With Al, baby. He's such a doll baby. He has to put on that gruff appearance so they don't take the ground from under him.

Dee: They took it out from Willie years ago . . . I feel so sorry for Willie now. He worked so hard. And it's all over. We have nothing but third place.

**Beside the player's entrance at Three Rivers Stadium, the wives have a sitting room for their exclusive use. After the last game, a few women are waiting for their husbands to dress.**

Dee Stargell relaxes in an armchair. "I'm sleepy. I think it's the weather—the rain. Did anyone bring a bottle?"

"I guess I didn't do any positive thinking! We should have had a bottle for this, too." Ginny Giusti's afterthought.

"I was going to stop at the store."

Ann grabs a child. "I didn't even think about it. Do you know the Millers in New York?"

"You mean Sue?" Dee asks.

"Yeah . . ."

"I would rather root for a team where I didn't know anybody. I'll see you next year . . . hopefully . . . either way, we'll see the same people. The winter's going to be longer this year . . ."

"Do you realize we've gone the whole season without a baby shower? . . ."

"But Brenda May had one . . ."

"Maybe that's why we lost. No babies this year. Just one. Before we usually had two or three . . ."

"If I thought it would have helped, I would have had one. See if we can't muster up some babies over the winter, girls!"

"Should be able to . . . We've been practicing all summer . . ."

"Practice makes perfect." [*Laughter*]

"Did you hear about the trip to Africa? I'd like to go there . . ."

"I get scared of flying. It lasts for a couple of months and then it goes away. I don't mind flying with Willie. I just don't like going alone."

"That's the same way I feel . . . Just the thought of dying . . ."

"This is the most awkward feeling—just sitting here . . ."

"I feel that I'll be coming back tomorrow . . ."

"Tomorrow—when you come back . . . if you come back at all . . ."

"That's optimistic. You know *you'll* be back . . ."

"You'll be back! But will I be?"

"You never know what's going to happen."

"I hate to think of sitting in a new club and looking at all new wives. Last year—we were sitting around saying you're going to be here and I'm not going to be here. Who would have thought it was going to be Clemente? I could be dead next year."

"Remember that four-to-one game? I've been remembering that game for a week . . ."

"Which one?"

"The one the Mets won in the ninth . . ."

"We lost a lot of games like that this year. I remember when we were leading seven to one and lost."

"Do you remember that far back . . ."

"We lost eighty-two games . . ."

"I keep thinking: If only . . ."

"We'll come back . . ."

"Remember when Baltimore won three straight. Then they were out for a year. They came back . . ."

"I felt funny like that last year in Cincinnati and we lost. Then we had to go home and there were no more games. 'Cause we were right in the thick of things. But now I don't feel so low this year. I'm just glad it's over with . . ."

"We sort of eased into it. We knew about three days ago what was coming. You could see it . . ."

"Yeah. You could see a steady drop. One day I looked and we were in third place . . ."

"Since Friday, it's been a countdown to nothing . . ."

"I didn't think there'd be so few trades, last year . . ."

"I can remember you saying—"How can they make it without trading?"

"A ballclub never makes it without trades . . ."

"Who went last year?"

"Davillo's with Oakland and Miller with the Mets."

"I felt sorry for Davillo when he left. Now look where they are. They were traded and they're the only ones in the play-offs!"

**After losing to San Diego and dropping to third place, Pittsburgh's final position in the Eastern Division, Willie talks in the locker room.**

Willie: The paper said this morning that Blass was responsible for us losing, but I have to tip my hat to Steve for the way he handled himself this year. He could very easily have said that his arm was bothering him, but he never alibied. Younger guys have watched him to see how he responded; they've been able to learn something from the way he dealt with his problems. Everybody wants to be a success, but at a low point, Steve never went down. He never complained.

I think if you got Steve stoned, or got him on a couch and gave him tranquilizers, if you could interview him subconsciously, you would find that each time he goes out there he really tries to help us. When we won the World Series, I remember what he said. He was so happy that he made a contribution because he didn't do nothing in the play-offs.

Now that Steve has not had the year he would liked to have had, he doesn't feel he can be part of that good feeling you have with the other guys. We see each other every day—we become like a family away from home. To be around each other and look each other in the eye is probably the hardest thing we have to do. More than going out there and playing. You do not know who is in the stands from one night to the other, but you know you got to see the players every day. You got to travel with them. You got to sit and play cards and take your clubhouse joshing. That Steve couldn't feel a part of us probably hurt him more than anything else.

The best thing for Steve now is rest. Sometime while he is cutting his lawn or painting the house, he can think about what has happened. If it's on the negative level, that is the time to bring it out in his own mind and spread it on the table. Examine just what the hell has gone on. You can also develop a positive way of dealing with your problems.

If someone told Steve to retaliate, he probably made the biggest mistake of his career. Or this year. If it was strongly suggested that *I* hurt or harm someone else, I couldn't do it. I wouldn't, but I would have more satisfaction not doing what I was told than doing what I was ordered to do.

When you're around the game for along time, guys go around every day saying, "If some son of a bitch throw at me, I want my pitcher to protect me. If you don't, then I ain't gonna play for you." If a guy throws at one of our guys, then a pitcher feels he's letting the team down by not retaliating. That becomes confusing. I am still surprised Steve could get so far off base when someone told him to retaliate. All the time, deep down inside, Steve must feel that if he throws the ball hard and hits somebody right, he could very easily turn them into a vegetable or disabilitate them for life.

210

No one can know but Steve. He has hit guys all year. He would yell, "Watch out!" But out of the twenty guys he's hit, I'm sure he couldn't name one that he intentionally tried to hit.

Steve is a helluva dude as far as I'm concerned. There's been days when I wanted to run up and grab him and tell him, "Hey, I know exactly what you're going through because I have dealt with some real horseshit years." People that haven't, can't identify. I have. I know exactly what his real feelings are in terms of what his teammates are thinking and feeling. He knows behind his back they're buzzing. When they come out the next day and say something to him, he doesn't know which one is being honest and which one is sincere. Which one has just got through talking about you like a dog and now he's being nice to you. That's a helluva thing to deal with. That's why I have to admire him. Besides, he is a nice guy and *I* know how hard it is to be nice!

I would have liked to see Oliver get one hundred RBIs because he's a real competitive guy—a true athlete. I feel for Al when he don't produce, because he's so determined. If he gets hurt, like when he knocked himself out over at the first-base line, he is so determined that he doesn't even think about it. I said, "Hell, if that had been me, my lip would have been all over." But Al really drives. He's an honest-to-God, dedicated professional. He takes pride, not only in baseball, but in every little thing he does. Like he keeps a little chart on himself—the pitches he gets, what he does each time at bat. He knows what he wants to do and does it. But he only got ninety-nine RBIs this year.

It seems strange not to be doing nothing. It's an eerie feeling. Now we are no longer part of the goal we were striving for. We're just cut out. The last three years, we've been very fortunate. This year we went to hell. But whatever we did, we did together. We won together and we lost together. I can't even think about what happened now. I've got to come down from the season. I don't believe what has happened.

I could say it's been a tough year for us, but we went through the year never giving up on ourselves when so many people said we weren't going to do anything. We were ten and a half games out. Everybody thought that was the end of it, but we felt capable. We really believed down to today. Actually we feel fortunate, because three out of the last four years we've been a very busy team at this time of year.

We have a good, young ballclub. There is no reason why we can't plan ahead. We have nothing to be ashamed of. Everybody gave their very best. We lost. You have to give the Mets credit. They played outstanding ball.

From a personal standpoint, I did have an outstanding year. I'm thankful for what I've been able to do, but I would have traded that for a good year and a winning season. We have come to a quick, sudden halt and I feel lost.

# The Last Day

Willie: I was prepared for the big letdown after not getting the Most Valuable Player Award this year. I figured I could go to any sporting goods store and order me a hell of a plaque or trophy and inscribe it just as I wanted to. I would never condition my mind for the prize the way I did in 1971. I had high hopes then, because the sportswriters said the player who helped their team the most would win. I had a high percentage of run production and the Pirates had won the World Series.

I thought I had won in 1971. When the MVP announcement was made, I was in the hospital. It was like a ton of bricks hitting me. I was disappointed and let down. I got to the point where I didn't believe nothing. The sportswriters said that the voting was distributed among too many valuable Pirates. I thought: Go back to Cincinnati in 1970. They had Pete Rose, Tony Perez, Johnny Bench and Bobby Tolan. The prize went to Bench. So the writers can not tell me there were too many valuable Pirates. In 1970, there were *more* valuable Cincinnati Reds. That was some bullshit they tried to run at me.

I could not get upset this year like I did in '71. It was a shock, because I led both leagues in six different categories. Home runs, RBIs, doubles, slugging percentage, game-winning hits and extra-base hits. Seems like a guy could have any kind of year and be up in Utopia expecting nothing and wind up with the MVP award.

When you take my production and Pete Rose's production, he led both leagues in one area. Batting average. It stung a little more than I expected when they unanimously gave Reggie Jackson the Award in the American League. I had a much better year than Reggie, but then Ron Carew had a much better year than Pete.

Sportswriters have never said it was an Award to an exciting player. Pete Rose creates excitement, but so does Joe Morgan. And Joe Morgan's got to get the prize for production. Morgan hit more home runs than Johnny Bench. He had eighty-two runs driven in to Pete's sixty-four. Joe walked one hundred twenty times to Pete's something like sixty. Pete scored one hundred sixteen runs. Joe scored one hundred fifteen. Joe stole seventy-two bases to Pete's fifteen. Joe had more game-winning hits. If you take Pete out of the lineup for a month and then, another month later you take Joe out of the lineup, who did you miss the most? These qualities should go into picking the Most Valuable Player. Maybe they do give the award to a flashy player. But then, as far as I am concerned, the two most exciting players to watch in the National League are Willie Davis and Lou Brock. Willie Davis going from first to third. Even if you're running after a ball, you want to look to see this man in motion. And Lou Brock studying the pitcher when he is going to get on base somehow. That is excitement.

At one time, MVP meant that you had had one hell of a year and your record proved it. Like O. J. Simpson. All of his awards are deserving. He can honestly sit back in his rocking chair and say he put his stuff together with sacrifice and work. On that basis, there were two years I should have gotten the MVP. 1971 and 1973.

Supposing this year is better than it has ever been, and also suppose that the writers take it upon themselves to give the MVP to me. I will wonder: Are they giving it to me or do they feel sorry for me? At a later time in my life, I will look at that award up on the wall and say, "I don't know if I got it out of merit or out of sympathy."

I used to think the MVP was given to the most valuable player to his team. Now I hate to see some young guy coming along who puts it together one year and goes out there with high hopes. He will get turned off if he doesn't get the prize. Luckily I have never just turned off. I was clearly upset and I stated that I was upset and I meant it. At least this winter I have traveled and received Man of the Year Awards, Most Valuable Award dinners and many major baseball awards on production. I cherish these awards. The MVP has lost its taste for me.

I am glad I wasn't MVP. Maybe 1973 was not my best year. Even though I did lead the league in six categories, I can go higher.

There hasn't been a ceiling put on my production yet. I could have bigger and better years and set higher goals. Out of something bad, something good will happen. I feel disappointed now, but it won't have any effects on my tomorrow.

People say so many things about last season. It was Blass who messed us up some say. Other people think I messed up Robertson's mind by playing first base in spring training, so Robertson had to come in behind me. People say we lost because Clines hurt his leg in San Diego. That Roberto was no longer with us. If you look for excuses you can find them.

I will say that Bill Virdon's firing was the strangest thing I have ever seen. Bill had twenty-nine days to go before the end of the season, and all of a sudden, he is not with the team. Management said, "We're not going to trust you going down the stretch with this delicate team of horses." I am sure Bill would have liked to have said, "Well, we just didn't do it," or "We came back like gangbusters." He got caught short. We, the players, had confidence in Bill. We were like little boys coming to their father and saying, "All right, you take us home." Somewhere along the line, we were going to click. And then we didn't.

We should have an interesting year this year. It may be comical, but it will be interesting.

**David Litman talks about the 1974
contract negotiations.**

Litman:  I'm not sure I can figure out Willie's motives or his real desires. I'd like to go to arbitration. Brown offered one sixty-five and said we'd have to go elsewhere for more.

In arbitration, you present a signed contract and management and the player each present a figure. The arbitrators choose either figure and fill out the contract. All bets off. I have to try to psyche Brown and determine what he's going to come up with. Then I have to arrive at a more reasonable figure. If he gave one fifty and I came out with three hundred, we would have a contract for one fifty.

Willie said that arbitration would hurt Joe Brown. Brown told Willie it would be personally painful if he went to arbitration. Then he offered us one sixty-five.

I said, "Joe, you must understand that when I met with you yesterday, I told you everything that happened. We decided before we came in here that Willie could not take less than a hundred seventy thousand dollars." Brown said, "You'll have to get that from someone else." Brown then asked if he could talk to Willie alone and Willie said okay, so I left.

When they had finished talking, I asked Brown if they had talked about the negotiations and he said, "Yes." I told him I resented his doing this without my being present. Then Brown stepped out of the office.

I told Willie my reasons for the type of presentation that I made. Willie shushed me, because he is certain the room is bugged. He said, "Brown brought up certain things which I'll tell you about later." Willie was upset, but I didn't know why. I was concerned.

Willie and I went to the Allegheny Club for lunch and he said when he was younger and had financial troubles, Joe Brown used to give him money out of his pocket. It amounted to a couple thousand dollars. When Willie indicated gratitude, Joe said, "I want you to forget about this, because I have." Then he brought it up today. He said, "Remember how I took care of you." Willie was hurt. And here's the strange thing. He doesn't even come close to loving this man Joe Brown, but he was so badly hurt there were tears in his eyes. Willie says, "What I want to do, I would like to take one sixty-five and go to Brown and say, 'All right. Our slate is clean. I'm going to have this very great year and I don't want to hear about the debt again.' "

I don't know whether Willie feels that this is the way to handle the situation or if he is timid. I don't know if he truly believes this will give him emotional solace or if he fears going into arbitration. Also, I *want* to go to arbitration. I've been hyping myself up. I want to take off my gloves and scratch eyes. I said to Will, "I would like you to come out standing tallest.

You know, if we find out that other ballplayers get one ninety, two hundred thousand dollars, I want to know how you will feel in May and June. You've always felt inferiority when you found out certain players were making more than you."

It seems to me that Willie is rationalizing. He's thirty-three. He's got to make the break now. A slugger can never be sure that he's going to have a good year, because his timing has to be so perfect. Willie can hit .265 easily as .300. He can hit twenty home runs as easily as forty. In spite of the fact that he had a good year last year with his knees, he could have a bad knee on that damn Astro turf.

I can push Willie, but I don't know whether I should. We can agree to go for arbitration. We can sign. We can do neither and hold out. Or Willie could go to the press and say, "I didn't go to arbitration, because Joe Brown came to me personally and asked me not to. Now he wants to give me one hundred sixty-five thousand." The code is over. In a year or two all the salaries will be out, but Willie still keeps to the rules. He can't seem to break that paternal tie.

Principle is important to Willie. And it's his psyche. How will he feel in the middle of the summer? Or next year? I don't know. I think he was the most valuable player in baseball last year. You don't often find a guy who leads the majors in five different areas and sets records in two of them. In addition to setting this town on fire civic-wise. Willie's loved and respected by everybody. He's the great Pittsburgh hero.

You can't imagine Willie going to Brown and getting angry: "Look, mother-fucker. This is where the fuck you're getting off." He's not going to do that. He'll say, "All right. I'll take it." He's going to be as mild-mannered as can be.

I'm troubled. This is my terrible kick—I get into clients' skins. Kick them out of their own skin. I do what I think is best for them. I dig too deep. Often I come on so strong I frighten my clients. But between Brown and Stargell, Stargell has to win. Brown wouldn't dare play brinksmanship with Stargell. Willie Stargell is more important to Pittsburgh baseball than Joe Brown is. If Hebner could have Virdon fired, Stargell could have Brown fired. Nobody likes Hebner. Everybody loves Stargell.

**Willie and Litman meet.**

Litman: I can only tell you what's best for you financially. I am totally satisfied that if you go into arbitration, you will get more money. And I should tell you that the amount of money you get next year will be based upon what you got this year . . . I just want to tell you. I was getting a bit too paternal or protective with you. Trying to get underneath your skin. But no question that you know what's best for your relationship with the team.

Willie: It's not relationship. I found out yesterday that I didn't have the relationship I thought I did. Brown just wants to get a ballplayer for the lowest amount he can. But I've thought about it and I'm going to forego arbitration. Brown feels I owe him a debt. If he feels that way, I want to get this debt over with now. I'll take one sixty-five and he'll have to pay the extra for my suite in hotels. (Willie has always lived in suites, but paid the difference himself.)

**Stargell signed a contract for one hundred sixty-five thousand dollars on the following Monday and left for spring training.**